Healing Improv
A Journey Through Grief to Laughter

BART SUMNER

Copyright © 2014 Bart Sumner

All rights reserved.

ISBN: 1496119711
ISBN-13: 978-1496119711

DEDICATION

For my parents, who taught me Love.
For Leslie & Abby, who feed me Love every day.
For David, whose legacy proves Love never dies.

CONTENTS

ACKNOWLEDGMENTS	i
DAVID'S LAST PRACTICE	1
"I CAN'T IMAGINE"	20
TELLING ABBY	23
ANGER	30
PULLING THE PLUG	34
TWO POEMS FROM A DARK PLACE	40
THE GROCERY STORE	43
ALLOWING OTHERS TO HELP	47
I READ THE NEWS TODAY, OH BOY	51
THE VEIWING & FUNERAL	61
LAST TIME THROUGH THE DRIVE-THRU	69
BUT HE DOESN'T KNOW ANYBODY	74
SPEAK HIS NAME, PLEASE	79

A TEAM MOVES FORWARD	83
IN MY DREAMS	87
FALLING	91
WHAT SHE LOST	97
PROTECTION IS A FANTASY	103
TWO CARS	108
BIRTHDAYS	111
GETTING OUT OF DODGE	115
LETTING GO OF EXPECTATIONS	121
IMPROV SAVED ME	126
HEALING IMPROV	130
THE 1ST WORKSHOP	138
FINAL THOUGHTS	144
APPENDIX - HEALING IMPROV GAMES	146

ACKNOWLEDGMENTS

Thank you to all the teachers and improvisers I have ever worked with. You taught me to laugh and be selfless and share myself. Without your humor and patience I would not be able to pass on the joy and power of improv.

DAVID'S LAST PRACTICE

> *Peter:*
> *"Forget them, Wendy. Forget them all. Come with me where you'll never, never have to worry about grown up things again."*
> *Wendy:*
> *"Never is an awfully long time."*
> *~J.M.Barrie - Peter Pan*

    It was not unlike any other night at the football field. Clear skies. Fall air that goes from 86 degrees to a brisk 68 degrees in about 30 minutes as soon as the sun slips away. The field had been there for years, nestled behind an old high school that today serves as an adult school, and up against the back a local neighborhood. In fact our cheerleaders, all sweet girls of 6-9 years of age, had gotten in trouble a week or so earlier for throwing rocks into the backyard of one of the houses. Kids will be kids.

    The field has a solid place in our little town's history. Many who guide and coach the youth football players that filled the field played there in their youth. There were stories of how the telephone poles that hold the field's lights used to be closer to the sidelines, and used to have old tires around them to keep players from killing themselves when they ran into them. Those old tires must have worked, because until what was going to happen around 7:20 that night, no one playing football here had ever died.

My wife, Leslie, was at the field at the top of practice. She and our daughter, Abby, were going to leave and go run an errand and get some dinner. She had lingered a while that night, watching our boy David go through the drills. As always, we cheered him on as he ran laps. He was never the fastest kid out there, but he never walked. Everyone within earshot knew how hard he was working to run those laps as he whined and grunted his way around the track. I have been told that while he ran he often repeated to himself "I can make it." And he always did. In his first season I didn't know what to make of his crying as he ran the field. But in the course of his football seasons, David had found his stride. The whine and cry had morphed more into a mantra for David. In fact the coaches used to tell us "If David's not making noise, he's not working hard." He let the frustration out as he ran, but he never stopped. As his team finished out the season after his death, his Coach told me that practices didn't seem the same anymore, because David's sound was absent from the field, and it just didn't feel right.

David had become a decent runner. He now typically finished in the middle to the back end of the main pack of runners. He was never last this year, not even close. His once pudgy and untested body was now very strong and in good shape. He pushed himself harder than we ever pushed him, but we would always shout encouragement to stay tough and catch those guys in front of him. One of David's teammates had told his dad that he hated it when I would cheer for David to catch him as they ran. His dad explained that it gave David a goal, which he always responded to. He told him it also meant that he too would then work harder, because he didn't want David to catch him, which would make David work harder, and so on, and so on. Explained that way, he got it.

That night David didn't disappoint, he finished hard and strong, and when they broke for water he strode over to his bottle, being cool and confident in a way that only David could. Never cocky or boastful, David was sure of himself and everything around him. He knew his place here. He knew what they expected of him. He would stand, as he always did during practice, hands folded in front of him, patiently waiting to be told to go get 'em. Leslie told him she and Abby were going to be leaving, he said "Okay." David gave her a hug. I'm sure if she had had even the slightest premonition of what was going to happen in about an hour, she would have held him tight and never let go. It's funny, we used to jokingly sing Sergio Mendes' "Never Gonna Let you Go" with the kids as they grew up. It was an old family joke by now, with both David and Abby fighting to get away from our grasps as we changed the lyrics of the song to "...gonna try and make up for the times we TICKLED you so," and then tickle them until they could barely stand it. David had gotten big and strong enough that if he had wanted to get away he could have, but he'd always wait for the tickling to start before he ran.

So David ran back to the coaches, the first player back on the field, and Leslie wrangled up Abby and off they went. As the sun dipped below the horizon, the orange hue to the west gave way to purple and blue hues as the vapor lights atop the dreaded telephone poles snapped to life, and the stars started to peek through the veil of darkness.

This particular night, practice revolved around a new makeshift offense. Our quarterback's shoulder was injured, and he was going to miss the game on Saturday. The coaches were desperately trying to devise a running game diverse enough to keep the other team guessing as to what plays we were running. David had been thrilled the night before to be given the role of rolling out with the receiver and blocking down field on a newly designed screen-pass play. David thrived on new plays. He knew the playbook backwards and forwards. He had been labeled "Coach" by his coaches two seasons ago. The nickname had followed him to baseball too. "Coach" was always thinking. In the huddle, if the coach made a mistake while calling a play David always corrected them. And they listened to him, they knew he'd be right. This year on the way home from the field with the new playbook, we weren't more than 300 yards down the road when David announced from the back seat, "Hey Dad, hear this, they have a mistake on page 23. It's says it's a 34, but it's diagramed like a 35." He sent the coaches an email when we got home, and of course he was right.

So there they stood tonight, in formations, going over what everyone's job was on the new plays. I could see after the coach would talk to David's side of the line David always turned to his teammates and confirmed what they had heard. David was probably double-checking to make sure he had heard the coach correctly, but what he was doing without realizing it was leading. By making sure he understood what the coach had said, he was making sure they all knew. This was the experience of a "veteran" player. He was a starter. He was coaching. After checking with the other players, he'd stand there politely with his hands grasped together in front of him waiting to be told what to do next. This went on for about an hour. The sky got darker, the lights brighter, and the air crisper. I put on my black sweatshirt from last year with his name and number "18" on it to keep warm. I must have put it on backwards because later that night, as I stood in the hallway outside the operating room where David was, someone would point out it was on backwards. Figures.

Around 7:10, the offensive play drilling was done, and the players were divided up to do the "alley" drill. The kids and the parents all seemed to wake up a little. There was going to be some fun in football practice tonight after all.

The "Alley" Drill is very similar to a kickoff. Two players stand about 30 yards away from two other players. The "Alley" between them is only 10 yards wide. The ball is thrown from one end to the players at the other. The goal is for the 2 offensive players to score, and the two defensive players to stop them. The players loved this drill. It gives everybody a chance to do everything. The first few rounds

David wasn't pushing himself. On his second turn, after missing a tackle, he looked at me and shrugged his shoulders. I gave him the "hang in there," "be tough," "focus on your target," sign language we had developed over the years. The next time down the alley, he made the play. He took down a teammate with a strong, around the waist tackle. Perfect football. He hopped up and looked my way. I gave him a silent cheer with my arms raised, and he gave me his trademark confirmation that all was okay; his right hand shot out and his thumb stood tall.

David had started flashing "The Thumb" a few years back during baseball. It was his way of saying, "I hear you. I'm good. Please shut up and don't embarrass me." It had become the thing we looked for, and he knew it. He got back in line.

A few more rounds and David stood poised to be part of the receiving duo. He was across the field from me and would be running towards me. I turned jokingly to another dad, "I think David would be fine if they never threw the ball to him on this drill." He laughed. His son was a good 6 inches taller than David. They had played together 2 years ago, and then his son moved up to the next division. David stayed an extra year in the lower division. This season they were playing together again, and they were the heart of the offensive line on the right side. We joked about David and his son as "The Fire Hydrant and the Telephone Pole." We both knew our sons weren't the best on the field, but we loved seeing the boys play, and encouraged our sons to be their best. He and I had connected during our first year on the sidelines together. It had been a tumultuous year, and we had bonded. We enjoyed each other's company. It didn't matter he was more of a blue-collar guy, and I was this weird artsy actor. What mattered was how we saw our sons, and what we wanted to instill in them as young men. We had figured out fatherhood in similar ways.

The ball flew down the alley, and went right to David. He knocked it to the ground, and quickly got a handle on it.

He started to run and moved in behind his blocker. Both defensive guys converged on David. His blocker threw a big block, and tied up both players momentarily. David adeptly stepped to the sideline, and then he was in the clear. It took a beat for everyone to realize that David was running for daylight. The coaches and parents erupted, as did the players.

"Go David!"

I leaned forward and yelled "Run Pal! Run!"

I could see as he came towards me that David was smiling under his helmet from ear to ear. As the team cheered on David, I saw one of the defenders get to his feet. This kid was one of the players David really looked up to. Talented and strong and just like David he never quit. David always knew when he came up against him that if held his own he had accomplished something. David could not outrun him, but he might just have a big enough lead to reach the…nope. Tripped up at the last minute by the shoelaces. David's feet stopped moving and he went down like a tree in the forest.

You had to have known David. He never really "fell" well. His reaction was always a little slow in protecting himself. Learning to ride his bike, he was always a little slow when he started to go down. Heck, I remember one time how glad I was he always wore a bike helmet as he fell over sideways and smacked the helmet to the street. He was fine that time thanks to the bike helmet, not his great reflexes. In football David had learned he was protected with the best equipment available, including a new helmet that was touted as state of the art at protecting players from brain injuries. So, wanting to make sure he didn't fumble, as he went down to the ground he covered up the ball and just went down, face first.

It's ironic, because every once in a while, to boost excitement, the coaches would run an "end zone dance" drill. The goal was simple, take the ball, run over the goal line and do your end zone dance. The kids loved this, always doing crazy dances, and just being kids. The first time David did it, he ran into the end zone, and instead of dancing like a lunatic, he stopped and fell forward to the ground, like a tree in the forest. He had gotten a laugh when he did it, and from then on, whenever they did that drill, it's exactly what he did every time. And we always laughed.

I cringed a little, even as I cheered in exasperation that he had not quite made it to the end line. David had gone down hard. Everyone else laughed and cheered the hard work by all involved. For a moment I thought, "Is he okay?" Then David popped up, and flipped the ball to coach. He turned to me and instantly gave me "the thumb."

"I'm okay Dad."

But I wanted to make sure. I always erred on the side of caution.

"You okay?"

He nodded and yelled back.

"Yeah, I'm fine."

Okay, so here is where tons of the second-guessing of how you could have done something to prevent it and protect your child comes in. See, I should have known that he popped up quickly because the fall was hard, and he was being tough.

I should have called him over.

I should have checked his eyes.

It was completely unnecessary based on what had just happened, but I should have known. Of course, if I had done any of those things, it would have changed nothing. Even if there were a way to know he had just injured his brain so badly that in a matter of twenty minutes he would close his eyes for the last time, it would have made no difference. My brother, a physician, later told me even if there had been a neurosurgeon on the sidelines, it would not have made any difference. From that moment forward, whether it was that tackle, or something else that had happened earlier on the field, David's fate was sealed. Things would unfold inside his head so quickly that they could not be stopped.

My boy was already gone.

David smiled, proud of what he had just done.

"Good run, pal!"

He gave me another thumbs up.

"Now go get me a tackle!" I urged him on.

He turned and got back in line. For the next 2 or three minutes another dad and I joked about our sons. I admitted I was glad that last fall hadn't hurt David. We cheered them on, and enjoyed being dads. Then David was up again, this time to go make that tackle on defense.

"Go get'em Pal!"

David took off as soon as the ball was thrown. He got about 15 yards down the field, and he went down. The other dad and I laughed. After that great run on the play before, it now looked like David had tripped in a divot on the field. We chuckled.

"Get up pal!"

One other thing you have to know about David; He always got up. So no sooner had he hit the ground, he was working on getting back on his feet. David pushed himself up, and then his right leg seemed to give out on him.

"Oh no he's hurt his knee." I exhaled under my breath.

I was out of my chair and moving towards him, as were several of the coaches. Like I said, David always got up. By the time I got to his side David was on his back, and his favorite coach was checking his knee and leg. David was a bit frantic. He was crying, not because he was hurt, but because he was anxious; he was experiencing something he could not explain.

David had a real emotional trigger. You could never tell when it might go off. It was always worse if he was tired or frustrated with himself. It was his first line of defense. It was the same thing that made him cry while running laps when he first started football. I recognized it and spoke as gently and calmly to him as I could. My immediate goal was to calm him down enough so he could help us help him with whatever was hurt.

David started to breathe deeply and started answering our questions.

"Where does it hurt?"

"It feels funny."

"Can you feel me touching your leg?"

"Yes, but I can't... it feels funny."

This is not good. Call Leslie.

I looked David in the eyes. "I'm gonna go call your mom pal, I'll be right back."

David nodded. "Mom. Yeah, get Mom dad."

He was scared; I could see it in his eyes. I got to my feet and crossed the field quickly to get my cell phone. Another coach called out to me, "I'm calling 911!"

I threw him the "thumb."

"Please!"

People were asking me questions, but I was focused on one thing, Leslie. I grabbed my phone and as I headed back to David I dialed her cell phone.

"I.C.E." "In Case of Emergency"

That's what always showed up on my screen when I called her. It was something I had read online, put your emergency contact under ICE, so if you are in a car accident they know whom to call. It was some unwritten code to paramedics and police. This was the first time the label was appropriate.

Voice mail. Shit.

There were now a few other coaches, some with more medical experience around. I knelt down next to David, he was breathing fast, and it looked like he was going into shock. I kept talking to him. "Hang in there pal, we're gonna take care of you. Just hang in there and breathe easy." I rubbed his thigh to let him know I was with him. I wanted to remove his helmet but they said no. A blanket came in from somewhere and they draped it over him. The sound of the emergency squad siren pulling into the field made me turn my head. They were here in three minutes; they literally were around the corner. Then I heard some one say, "David stay with us."

I turned back to see David blinking his eyes. I got down right next to him. "David. David, stay with us Pal."

"Stay With Us!"

"DAVID!"

His eyes fluttered. His eyes rolled back a little, and his lids closed. I have no idea whether he heard me then, or while we kept talking to him. I don't know. For all I know he's watching me cry as I write this. But I don't know. What I do know is that then and there, David was gone.

Never again would I hear his voice, or his laugh, or his cry, or that stupid fart noise he used to do so well on his arm. I would never feel his hug again. It was done. That moment will haunt me for the rest of my life.

I am comforted that I was with him. I know that he was less afraid because I was there. But I saw the joyous little soul I had helped nurture go away from this world. And though I know it calmed him and reminded him how much he was loved, it has forever changed me.

My boy was gone.

Call Leslie.

I stood up as they cut away David's jersey and pads, and slid his helmet off.

Voice mail again. SHIT.

I put the phone in my pocket. The EMS truck pulled out onto the field, and pulled right next to David. I heard the "Monday Night Football" theme ringing in my pocket.

Leslie.

"Honey, David's hurt, there's an emergency crew at the field. Come now."

I don't know if that's exactly what I said, but I remember hearing her fly into a panic and bolt for the door.

The next 10 minutes were a blur. I kept talking to David who started to have a seizure, twisting and turning, fighting whatever was going on in his brain. I grabbed his hand.

"I'm here Pal. I got you. Keep fighting."

The EMS crew asked questions, and tried to assess what they were dealing with. His weight? 100.

No allergies.

No diabetes.

No health issues.

He went down while running.

He fell a little hard on the play before.

They gave him an injection to help with the seizure. I held down David's arm. "A seizure, oh God, let it just be some kind of seizure!" They decided to put a collar on him and get him on a backboard. I stood up; parents hugged me and offered support. Leslie arrived.

Leslie was running out to the field, Abby trying to keep pace. Leslie yelled at Abby to stay put and ran towards me. I quickly explained what was happening. One of us can go to the hospital in the ambulance.

"You want to go?" I asked.

"Yes."

"I'll get Abby and meet you there."

"I think I scared her."

"I've got her, you worry about David." I turned and went to Abby as they loaded David into the EMS truck.

Abby was crying so I picked her up. I immediately thought of the time I had carried David through the parking lot of the emergency room we were now headed to. He had awoken from a nap and had trouble breathing. It had been only a scare, they treated him and he had a quick recovery that time. This time I was not so sure.

I told Abby we were going to go to the hospital.

"David's hurt badly, but the ambulance is going to take care of him and we'll meet them at the hospital."

She was scared. I was scared. We grabbed our chairs and David's gear and threw them in the SUV. We climbed in, buckled up and pulled out to follow the EMS truck. Immediately I cut someone off and nearly caused an accident.

Sorry.

"Slow down Bart. You need to get to the hospital safely. Abby is in the back and she's counting on you." I said to myself.

"Take care of Abby."

That has become my mantra since David died, and that ride to the hospital was when it started. Leslie and I have always been honest with our kids. So honest that people often felt we told them too much. Like a year earlier, when our neighbor decided to kill himself in the RV parked next to our yard. We knew that David and Abby were going to hear things in the neighborhood, so we sat them down and explained it to them. We told them it was very sad. That he had been in lots of pain, and he was not thinking straight. He had shot himself, which is why guns are dangerous and never to be played with. They understood as best they could and never asked another question about it. We have always given them the respect we ourselves would want. Protect, but be truthful about life and what goes on. So here I was with Abby. I would need to choose my words carefully. I wanted nothing in the world more than to make her unafraid by promising David was going to be fine, because that was what I wanted to tell myself. But I knew I couldn't do that, this was an important "rest of her life" type moment.

I told her we were going take the best care of David we could.

I did not tell her everything would be okay, or that David would be okay. I simply told her we were doing the best we could to help him. I have no doubt that it scared her. She didn't really understand what was wrong, hell, none of us did, but she knew it was serious, and that she should pray for her brother. I believe that it prepared her for what she would hear the next morning in the garden in front of Children's Hospital. She probably ran it around her mind that night when she went to bed at our neighbors. And she prepared herself for the fact David might really be hurt. I doubt she entertained the idea that her big brother would die, but she was braced, at least on some level, for bad news.

I arrived at the emergency room with Abby. I called our neighbors who had quickly become our best friends in town, and whose 2 kids were the same ages as David and Abby. I told her what had happened quickly, and could she come get Abby for us. Without hesitation she assured me not to worry about Abby, just worry about David. I went into the emergency room and left Abby in the lobby watching TV.

The nurses were hurriedly hooking David up to all sorts of machines. They were asking all the same questions again. Leslie and I were at David's side, answering all the questions, and talking to him in between. It's one of those times when you are desperately looking for some sign from the people who know what's going on to give you some clue to what's going on. It didn't help that there were not a great deal of reassurances being offered up, but hell, they were working really hard to do what they could for him. Leslie was worried about Abby, and wanted to tell her she loved her before our neighbor got there, so she went out quickly to the lobby to be with her.

I sat down next to David and started talking to him. I told him everybody was doing everything they could for him. I told him if this was some kind of a joke, it wasn't funny. I promised him that if he'd just open his eyes and talk to me, we could go to McDonalds and he could get whatever he wanted. The nurse checking his IV heard this and smiled at me.

I noticed David was starting to turn blue. I stood up to tell someone, but the equipment they had hooked him to had already alerted the staff. Before I got to them, they were in the room. I got to watch them "intubate" him, which I had seen done a thousand times on "ER," and knew it wasn't good.

Leslie returned from the lobby, our neighbor had arrived and taken Abby home with her. The staff came in and rolled David out to take x-rays. I needed air, and needed to speak with my brother the doctor. Maybe he would have something I could grasp onto for reassurance. Leslie sat down to wait for David to come back from x-ray.

I stepped outside to find the entire football coaching staff hanging around the doors, smoking. They looked devastated and worried. "Join the club," I thought sarcastically to myself. I quickly told them what was happening and then called my brother. My brother instantly knew this was serious, but he has always been very measured in his responses, and he tried as best he could to remain professional and calming. But the one thing he couldn't do was assure me David was going to be okay. That seemed to be a disturbing trend with everybody involved. After I hung up with him, I needed to talk to my parents. It's fascinating, even though I was 45 years old, when the proverbial crap hit the fan, like all of us, I still needed my mommy and daddy.

But in my head this call terrified me as well. When I was a young man, I had wanted to play football. My parents, who had seen a family friend's son break his knee twice while playing high school football, told me "No." They told me I wasn't tough enough and that you could get hurt playing football. I have always joked that I got even with them for that by joining the drama club and becoming an actor instead. When they visited the year before, we had gone to the field, and my dad had commented several times about how hard they were working those poor little kids. He even had said it to David, who with his usual charm had told my dad that it was okay because he loved it. Now, I had to call them and tell them their grandson was in the emergency room having his head x-rayed because he was unconscious and on a breathing machine. Not your typical friendly call. They of course were nothing but supportive and concerned. I could hear my mother fighting to hold back the tears as I broke down on the phone with them. They immediately decided to come out to California from Florida. When we hung up, I got myself composed and headed back inside.

David was just coming back from x-ray as I got inside. Leslie and I were both trying to find out what they thought was going on, but no one wanted to say. They assured us that a neurosurgeon was on the way to the hospital and would be there very soon. As time ticked by and we sat vigil next to David, we grew anxious wondering what was taking so long. It really wasn't very long at all, but when your child is lying there unresponsive, time moves very slowly, and nerves get short and it takes everything you have to hold it together.

By now I knew we were losing him. I hadn't said it out loud to Leslie, and kept telling myself not to think that way, but I knew this was not going end well at all. I kept telling myself, "No stinking thinking," a phrase we used with the kids to drive home that they needed to keep a positive attitude in life, but I knew this was bad. Of course when the neurosurgeon arrived, any doubts I had about the situation evaporated completely. They handed him the x-rays as he strode into the room and as he looked at them there was no doubt he knew every second mattered. He started barking orders to the staff to get David moving towards the operating room. When they didn't move fast enough, saying they needed to get the IV ready to move him, the neurosurgeon himself grabbed the foot of the hospital bed and started to roll him out. I believe his statement was, "I don't give a damn about the IV, get him moving, NOW!"

They rolled David out, and Leslie and I stood there.

So where do we go now?

The waiting room for surgery was a small room, about ten by fifteen feet with several of the wooden armed, fabric-seated chairs you find in most office waiting rooms these days. They weren't overly comfortable, but not horrible either. Of course the last thing on our minds was how comfortable the chairs were. Our son David was in surgery to fix whatever was going wrong inside his head. They had told us it was a "subdural hematoma." After talking with my brother the doctor, I knew that meant his brain was bleeding, but more than that, we didn't know.

It was late in the evening, so thankfully we were the only people waiting on surgery. Lew, our local pastor, who knew David because he had served as acolyte numerous times on Sundays, was now with us in the waiting room. He was a real down to earth guy, and other than leading a prayer for God to watch over David, didn't push any heavy religious message. He knew being here with us, in case we needed to fall apart, or wanted the full court religious press, was his role. He was comforting, and soothing, and though I don't count myself as especially religious, it was nice to have a representative on our team, just in case. Also with us now was one of our family's best friends. He loved David dearly, and was Abby's godfather. I had called him earlier because our kids were the closest thing he had to kids of his own, and I knew he'd want to be here if he wasn't out working in his limo. He had dropped everything and come immediately.

Now the four of us sat in this tiny room. Silently. Waiting.

Every possible scenario ran through my head. One of the nurses downstairs had said there was already brain damage happening before they had rolled him off to surgery, so I knew that was on the table. I hoped it would not be too severe and with some rehab perhaps he'd be okay. Maybe by some miracle the nurse was wrong, doctors got this kind of thing wrong all the time, and he'd emerge fine. Or maybe it was serious brain damage, and our wonderful boy would never be the same. To be completely forthcoming, it ran across my mind that if the brain damage was going to be so severe that he would be seriously handicapped, then maybe it was better if the universe took him back. I don't know if I could have handled seeing his wonderful mind and spirit injured to a point he was only merely surviving. And of course there was the possibility that this was it, he would not be any of those things, and our boy would be gone.

I called my folks again, by now they had plane reservations for the morning and were packing to leave for the airport. I called our neighbor to check on Abby. She had played and then gone to bed with the neighbors' kids. She was doing okay. So we waited. And waited.

Finally word came that the surgeon was coming out of surgery. The neurosurgeon working on David was not a pediatric neurosurgeon, but he was the only neurosurgeon that could get to David in time, so we were thankful. I was later told by the head of the ER that his actions that night were nothing short of heroic in stepping up. I was thankful he was willing to do whatever he could. Without him, David would have never had a chance.

They led us to a door outside the operating room. The first doctor through the door was not our neurosurgeon, but another doctor who had assisted. His expression was reserved and non-committal. He told us the doctor would be out in a second, and sure enough, moments later, out came our doctor. He was not smiling. As he came out he removed his little surgical cap and introduced himself. I guess bedside manner is not something neurosurgeons work too much on in medical school, but then again, the news we were about to get could not have been delivered in any acceptable way.

"He's not going to make it."

The words were like a two by four to the forehead.

As if she must not have heard him correctly Leslie asked, "What do you mean? What are the odds?"

"100% He's not going to survive."

As if that wasn't definite enough, he then explained the situation in graphic detail I will never forget.

"His brain strangled itself of oxygen because of the swelling. I tried to relieve the pressure as quickly as possible, and when we removed a piece of his skull to try and help, the brain pushed it's way out of the opening like a cauliflower. There was nothing we could do."

I always fucking hated cauliflower.

We were stunned. I asked Leslie if she needed to sit down, but her lioness instincts had kicked in, and she barked at me, "I do not want to sit down!" She needed to hear how this was already over.

"There is no brain function. The tissue is already dead."

We all stood there for a moment.

Then came the question I dreaded asking, but I had to know.

"Was there an injury we missed? Something that had happened before and we should have known not to let him on the filed?"

The doctor shook his head. "Not that I could see. It was all new blood. I saw nothing that indicated he had an older injury. We've got him on life support, and we'll monitor his vital signs, but right now there is no activity at all."

There was nothing more to say to us. He had been very definitive. The last thing he wanted to see was these two parents fall apart, he was ready to get out of there. I'm sure it was not a wonderful moment for him either. All his years of training and learning were powerless to fix what had happened. I'm sure as a neurosurgeon he had a bit of a god complex, at least the ones on TV always seem to have one, and he didn't want to hang around.

"I'm sorry," was all he said, and then he was gone.

Leslie spoke up to the other staff.

"Can we see him?"

I noticed at that moment that the other people on the hospital staff were fighting back tears. They were all in horrible pain over what had happened. I don't know whether the fact we had not fallen to the ground and wailed and made a scene made it worse, but they were in shock as well.

The nurse nodded. "Of course, they're cleaning him and the room up a bit, we'll come get you in a moment."

When they led us into the operating room, it was very clean. David laid in the middle of the room, ventilator and other equipment hooked up to him. Except for the large bandage he had wrapped around his head, and the large bulge where they had attempted to relieve the pressure, he looked like he was sleeping. I took his hand, and desperately searched for some kind of sign that the doctor must have been wrong. None came. The nurses choked back tears as they left us alone with him.

"Oh pal, I'm so sorry."

Leslie leaned over and kissed him.

We stood there, looking around the room, taking it all in, trying to figure it out. Tears were in our eyes now, but there were no grand theatrics. That wasn't our style. We knew we were both devastated; there was no need to prove it.

It was at that point we made a decision that many have praised us for. To us it seemed completely natural. I'm really not sure which one of us said it, and which one of us responded in the affirmative, but it came out in a very off-hand, matter of fact kind of way.

"I guess we donate his organs."

"Yup. He'd like that"

That decision was made. David would have liked that. He had always enjoyed making sandwiches after a holiday party and driving around town to share the food with homeless people in need. Or sharing his Halloween candy with the homeless; "One for me, one for the homeless bowl." He would have wanted to give. Though we have been praised for donating his organs, David made that decision easy.

Eventually we left him in the operating room, they were going to transport him to Children's Hospital in Los Angeles to wait and see if anything would change. Much of this time is a blur, but I know I called my parents and told them he was gone. And then I called our neighbor to tell her, and to please not tell Abby, Leslie and I wanted to tell her the next day, together. I will never forget the cry and howl of angst that she released on the other end of the phone when I told her David was gone. It was guttural and primal. We later would discuss how she had, just like us, run through all sorts of scenarios that night. How her kids would help nurse David back to health, and how we'd all get through it together. When I told her he was dead, it shattered everything for her. In hindsight, she did the howling for us all that night.

This was David's last practice. The night my boy died.

"I CAN'T IMAGINE"

Truer words have never been spoken.

I have spent my life as an actor and screenwriter putting myself in other people's situations, trying to bring honesty to the emotion and character. But until David died, I never truly knew what despair was. I think it's safe to say that people are not capable of imagining the horror of losing a child. Your mind will not let you go there. It's a self defense mechanism. I used to tell people, "Everybody's worse problem, is their worse problem," but I was wrong.

The list of feelings you subject yourself to when your child dies is endless. I'm sure there are many I still have coming to me, which will bubble up down the road and crush me like so many others have. But there's one I've tortured myself with, which though I have reconciled it away with logic and understand with all my being is not true, it still never goes away and will always eat away at me.

I'm a failure as a parent.

I mean really, how can you feel any other way? From the moment you hold your child for the first time, the very basic of all things is "keep them safe." Of course they are going to get hurt, break a bone or chip a tooth. That's to be expected. Kids will be kids. But at the very least the one thing you are supposed to do, is KEEP THEM ALIVE. In this, I failed. I know things happen we have no control over. The universe is a chaotic place, and the very nature of life is that it is tenuous at best, and none of us get out alive, but that doesn't change the fact my child, who I was entrusted with at birth, died. That fact upsets the entire balance of the natural order of things. No matter how much love and understanding you shared with your child, no matter how wonderful they were with other children, or caring to those in need, or talented, or sweet and funny because you gave them all the right lessons and instilled all the right values. He died. I failed.

Perhaps it's this most epic of realizations that makes it so difficult to hear all the things people say to try and help. Without knowing what a person's personal beliefs are, so many people offer up a litany of platitudes designed to "Make us feel better." "He's in a better place." "God had a plan." "Only the good die young." "He gets to see Jesus every day." I know why people offer these thoughts up. It's because they can't fully wrap their heads around what you've told them. Losing a child is such a crushing thought to people, that they struggle to say something worthy of the tragedy. What they don't realize is that there is nothing that has ever been written or said that can help us "get over it."

We all get through it however we can. Every person deals with grief in his or her own way. For me, I needed to find something to say to all the anemic attempts at comfort, which would not insult the person, but would help them see that they don't understand. One day it just popped out of my mouth. A good friend who loved my boy dearly, who had been very supportive uttered the "He's in a better place" line when grasping to find something to say. With tears in my eyes I simply said, "I guess you've never been in his room." The tears and look of recognition that came over their face told me that had done the trick. I've used it in different variations for all the well-meaning platitudes, sometimes using his video games or hugging his sister in place of his room. I don't use it in anger or malice, I just tell them matter of fact that what he had here, and the life he still had left to lead here with all the people that loved him, was what was meant to be. And that there is nothing that you can say that will make logic of it all.

Interestingly, the thing most people say after they realize the depth of the hurt is, "I can't imagine." I always smile at that and nod and assure them, "You're right. You can't. Neither could I until I was there. Thanks for understanding."

Because the truth is, we don't really want someone to "make it better." We want someone who will sit here and listen, even for a moment, as we slog through the grief, anger, and confusion of what has happened. Because the journey of grief is not something that can be fixed or made easier. It is a devilishly hard road that you must travel so you can arrive at the other side. Only then can we begin to live again, and hunger for the wonderful things life has to offer. For those that have not had to face that journey, the best thing you can tell anyone who is going through that tunnel of grief is "I can't imagine."

Because you can't, and we already know that.

TELLING ABBY

Perhaps the most difficult thing we had to do when David died was to tell his 7-year-old sister Abby what had happened.

Football had been a huge part of her life in the last few years. She would come with us to practices. She would play with the siblings of David's teammates during practices and pretty much had the freedom to run around the field with them and do whatever she wanted. A few times they got into trouble doing things they shouldn't have, but they were kids, everyone there knew to look out for them, and that was part of the fun of spending so much time at the football fields; the other families. She even joined the cheer squad one year, learning cheers to urge her big brother and his team on. I'm sure it wasn't always her favorite place to be, but most nights she had lots of fun at the field.

The night of the accident we had our backdoor neighbors pick Abby up from the hospital and take her with them for the night. She went to their house, one of her favorite places with her favorite people. I'm sure she was concerned for her brother, but she was with people that loved her, and things were as normal for her that night as they could be.

After our horror filled night in the hospital, we knew that we had to tell Abby that her brother wasn't going to be okay. We also knew this was something we needed to do together, both because neither Leslie nor I wanted to do it alone, and because she had to hear it from us, together, so she knew that we were all going to find our way through this together.

Overnight David had been transferred the 30 odd miles from our local hospital to Children's Hospital Los Angeles. Neither Leslie nor I got any real sleep that night, even though there were beds at the hospital for us to use, neither one of us slept much. We were exhausted, but somehow the idea of sleeping seemed wrong. Part of me still held out hope that maybe they were all wrong and David would show signs of recovery. I think I slept for maybe an hour before we got word David was now in a room, and we could go see him. We went to see him, and then we devised a plan to bring Abby down to the hospital so she could spend some time with her brother, see him, and start to understand what was happening. I decided to drive back to our home and get Abby. I called our neighbor, who was still in tears over the whole ordeal, and told her I would come get Abby before the kids left for school, and to please try to keep everything as normal as possible until I got there.

On my drive from the hospital, I needed food, so I pulled into a Burger King for breakfast. It actually brought an ironic smile to my face. The morning David was born, we were headed to the hospital for a C-section, and I knew it was going to be a long day, so even though Leslie could not eat because she was about to have surgery, we pulled through a McDonald's drive through to get me breakfast. It had always been one of those funny stories we told about the cruel mean husband (me) who cared more about his appetite than the fact his wife was about to give birth to their first child. Now, here I was in another fast food drive thru, only this time it was on the way to deliver devastating news to my little girl about her big brother. If you're wondering, I had 2 Sausage Egg & Cheese Croissan'wiches. Not exactly healthy, but the idea of staying on my diet was off the table for the next few days… weeks… months.

I pulled into our neighborhood, but before I went to get Abby I had a few things to do. I went home and called David and Abby's school. Being the ardent rule follower that my parents raised, I wanted to let them know Abby would not be at school for a few days, and well, David would not be coming back. I got the office on the phone and tried to tell them quickly what had happened without falling to pieces. I wasn't completely successful at that. The first woman I spoke to, who was fighting back tears, asked me to hold for a moment. The next person to pick up was the principle, and she was already in tears. I explained that it had happened at football practice and that I was sure there would be kids talking about it and they needed to be prepared. I got off the phone as quickly as possible.

I went upstairs to change my clothes and get Leslie some fresh clothes, and there at the top of the stairs was David's room.

I walked in and sat on his bed. I told him again I was sorry, and begged him to forgive me if we had missed something. I smelled his pillow. Through the tears I spied his favorite stuffed bear, a purple beanie baby with Randy Moss's number on it, #18. It was the same number David wore. It was a Viking's bear, the same name as the team David played for. I thought I should get that for him, and then it occurred to me Abby might like to help get his stuffed animals for him, so I left it where it was until she and I could come and get it.

I went into our bedroom gathered clothes in a bag, and called my best friend. He had been the best man at my wedding and I had "married" him and his wife in a mock ceremony at their wedding party for their friends. I told him David was gone. He and I had been through a lot over the years, but this was not something he was prepared for. I asked him to contact our friends and let them know what had happened. We cried. Again, I got off the phone as quickly as I could.

I headed downstairs to go and get Abby, but first did something I regret to this day.

I was reeling from the shock and pain, and I was angry at the world, and a part of me wanted to lash out at the world and let everyone know how cruel the world had been to us. So I sat down and posted a status update to Facebook. Yeah, I know, it was stupid and impulsive and I would get plenty of angst about it from Leslie, but the truth is Facebook would prove to be a great source of comfort and healing as time went on.

What I posted was short and direct: "Last night we had the most wonderful boy ripped from our lives. We will never be the same." I posted it and left. I regret doing it, because Leslie was not ready to announce it to the world. I figured the coaches knew by now, our neighbors and family knew, and I wanted to make as many people feel as miserable and horrified over what had happened as I felt. It was careless and thoughtless, and I have apologized for it many times. But once more for good measure; I'm sorry Leslie, I screwed up.

As I inched up the walk to our neighbor's house I could hear the kids playing inside. I rang the bell and Alicia and Matt came to the door. The look on their faces was one of horror, but I was damned and determined to keep it together until Leslie and I could speak to Abby together. I can't imagine what was in their minds, but they took their cues from me, and remained strong and supportive. There were no hugs, because we knew that would only devolve into tears. We quickly wrangled Abby, and she and I went on our way.

I told Abby that David was in Children's Hospital in Los Angeles, and asked her if she thought he'd like it if we brought him a couple of stuffed animals to keep him company. She liked that idea. We stopped home and got the "18" bear and another stuffed animal and headed off to drive down to the hospital.

She didn't ask me any hard questions, and I kept the conversation light and happy. I can honestly say it was the hardest 35-minute drive I have ever made in my life. As we got close to the hospital, I called Leslie and told her we were on our way. We had agreed to meet downstairs near the garden, and we could take her there and talk with her.

I parked the car, and we gathered up the stuffed animals and the bag of clothes and met Leslie at the front door. We told Abby we needed to speak with her before we went up to see David. Leslie gave her a big hug and kiss and we strolled into the small quiet garden.

We found a nice stone bench to sit on away from everyone else and sat down. We told her that David had been hurt very badly, and that the doctors said he was not going to survive. Tears instantly welled up in her eyes, but she blinked them back. We explained that his brain had been injured too badly, and he was never going to wake up. We told her he was in no pain, but there was nothing anyone could do and he was not going to be coming home again. All three of us fought back tears. We held her and kissed her, and told her we were very sorry, and that if there was anything we could do to change it we would, but there was not.

Abby then blinked away the tears again, and a moment of clarity came across her face. Like an old soul, she look at us both, and with a certain amount of wonder and inevitability our little 7-year old girl said, "You know, we were just talking the other day about what it must be like to be an only child. I guess now I'm gonna find out."

I wasn't sure before we told her that she was going to understand fully what we were telling her. Whether she could fully comprehend what had happened. But those words told me that she did. She was scared. She suddenly realized to a great degree, she was alone.

We asked her if she wanted to see David, and at first she was unsure. We explained that it was okay to be scared, but that it was just her brother. We told her she could talk to him if she wanted. She asked if he would be able to hear her, and we told her we didn't know, but we liked to think so.

We went up to the hospital room, and as we entered the glass walled room I could tell she was not sure what to do. We held her and told her it was okay to touch his hand, and did so to show her it was okay. I think for the first few minutes she was overwhelmed and a bit lost. She probably wanted to cry, or run from the room, but she hung in there, knowing that we felt it was important for her to be there, and I think she sensed it too.

Then, an angel in the form of a social worker came in from the hospital. She carried a small white box and some art supplies. This was after all Children's Hospital, and Abby was not the first little sister or brother suddenly faced with losing their partner in crime. She approached Abby and asked her if she'd like to make a special box for her and David, and showed Abby the markers and ribbon she had. She told Abby she could decorate it anyway she wanted.

Abby's eyes started coming back to life. This she understood. This was a way she could make sense of it all. She smiled. Excitedly she started picking out ribbon and colors and went to work making a box to remember David by. His favorite foods, her favorite foods, favorite movies, games, parents. It all went on the box. The woman even made handprints on paper of Abby and David's hands together, so she would always have his hand to see and hold.

This woman helped save Abby at the darkest moment.

Today, over 4 years since that horrible day, Abby still has that box in a special place in her room. Over the years there have been questions arise in her ever-maturing mind that didn't occur to her back then like, "Who knew David was dead before I did?" She never asks them out of anger, but when they occur to her she needs the answer, to know how it all went down. And on nights when she has trouble falling asleep right away because she's "thinking of David," she pulls out that same white box with all the writing of a brave little 7-year old girl, and reads all the things she put down on there. She keeps other memories of her brother in and around that box, and on nights she misses her best friend, she takes great comfort in having that box, and all those memories. She has confessed that she is afraid she is going to forget him sometimes. We hug her and tell her that's normal, many of the little things may fade away, they do for us too, but that she will never forget him, or his love. That always seems to help. She knows she is not alone in missing him.

    It helps me too.

ANGER

> *"Anger is an acid that can do more harm to the vessel in which it is stored than to anything on which it is poured."*
> ~ *Mark Twain*

These words by Mark Twain are absolutely true, but that doesn't take away the fact that when your child dies, anger is inevitable. I actually thought I knew what it meant to be angry before David died.

Like all of us, I had experienced flashes of anger in my life. I was not above the occasional angry colorful vulgarity or systematic flipping of "the bird" when cutoff on a freeway, or the frustrating anger at myself as I frantically ran around the house trying to find my keys when I was already late for something that at the moment seemed very important. I even had been known, and I know this is hard to believe, to lose my patience with my kids when they were not listening, or God forbid, just being kids. Of course, those moments have come back to me many times since my boy's death, the times I foolishly lost my temper over things that make no difference now. I have tortured myself with those moments where I was unfair to him, or hurt his feelings needlessly when I was the one at fault. How I wish I could go back and take every single one of them back. To hold him again and tell him I'm sorry for being human is something I will never have the chance to do. Think about that next time before you scream at someone. I know I do now.

In fact, after David's death I think it's safe to say that those particular moments of anger have faded away a great deal in my life. I still get annoyed, and have been known to raise my voice at Abby for not doing what I need her to do, but the idea of anger has forever been changed for me. I am much less likely to fly off the handle quickly. It takes all of her 11 year-old skills to push my buttons efficiently enough for me to blow my stack these days. It's not that I'm not capable of it anymore; it's just that I have been given a new perspective on what anger is.

The kind of anger that Mark Twain was talking about is not something I was overly familiar with before; anger that seeps down into your entire being. That kind of anger, which bubbles up from nowhere and turns everything you see and do into an infuriating experience, was something I only truly knew after David's death. I had heard tales of people standing in the wilderness, screaming at the universe over things that had made them angry. But to me that seemed so over the top, something that I could not imagine myself doing. I was wrong.

In the first year after David's death, it was not uncommon for me to drop Abby off at school and start to cry as I pulled out of the parking lot, and continue those tears all the way back home. Of course, by that point I would have the rage at life's injustice multiplying inside of me. I could quell the anger by playing music and diving into the pool of tears sometimes, hoping for an emotional release that would calm the rampant emotions, but other times the music was not enough to sooth my savage breast. I would instead walk into the living room of our house and fill the vaulted ceilings with the most unworldly sounds of pent up anguish and torment ever known to the human ear. I'm sure if anyone had walked by during my detonation of sorrow they would have called the police for fear someone was torturing some large wild animal with a taser gun in my living room.

I suppose if I were a religious person, the target of my anger would have taken the personification of God, but I was venting to a universe that I now finally understood was not fair. After all, my father had drummed into me "Who told you life was fair?" my entire life whenever I would dare say "That's not fair." He had raised me with an acute awareness that things were going to happen in life that just flat out suck. This was far above and beyond the kind of thing my father had been talking about, but it certainly fit this situation too.

I would shriek to the skies in a vain attempt to somehow rip an opening in the fabric of the space-time continuum and cause the days and weeks before to somehow go back to the way they were before. Like the implausible moment at the end of that Superman movie where he flies around the world counterclockwise, and sets the world spinning backwards to turn back time to save Lois Lane. I felt perhaps my bawling would make that happen. To be honest, at times I was surprised that the walls had not collapsed or the paint fallen from the ceiling as I remembered it did in the old gymnasium at Rutgers when the college basketball crowd really started chanting when I was a boy. But alas, the building remained standing, as did the realities of time and space.

I'm thankful I had a safe place to go and fume at the cosmos. I always felt a release during those tirades and, truth be known, they were essential to my survival. It's interesting to note, that this anger from David's death affected Leslie and I very differently. She was always the more patient parent with the kids, and often I would get "the look" if I got angry too quickly with the kids. After David's death Leslie was angry at the universe too, but whereas my anger seemed to subside in the day to day, saving up for my herculean outbursts, Leslie became short with everything. Her patience for the mundane and superfluous became palpable and immediate. I saw her anger spark much more readily. It was as if our boy's death had reversed our roles. As time went on, her anger has waned, as has mine. It's not that we both aren't still furious at all creation for taking David from us, it's just that we've spewed out much of the anger, and learned to let it go as best we can.

I still have days where I am angry and anxious at the world for no apparent reason. On those days I try to stay away from situations that will make me angrier, and often end up going to bed early, because a good night's sleep tends to reset the table. I have taken Mr. Twain's observation on anger to heart, and when it is consuming me from the inside out I find the most constructive ways for me to spill it out; to an empty house and uninterested universe.

Perhaps when it comes to anger an ancient Chinese saying is more appropriate, and can help those looking to understand the rage we feel as parents who have lost a child: "Anger is not only inevitable, but it is necessary. For in its place is indifference, the worst of all human qualities."

I don't know a single parent who is indifferent to losing their child, and the fact they no longer are there to love and hold. Anger is a necessity, how we "pour it out," to keep from eating ourselves alive, is our only choice in the matter.

PULLING THE PLUG

"Ever has it been that love knows not its own depth until the hour of separation."
~Kahlil Gibran

There is nothing that has ever been written, spoken or divined anywhere, that can prepare a person to make the decision we had to make. It had been less than 72 hours, not even three days, since David had fallen during practice and been torn from our lives. But here we were, gathered in a small room with the doctors who had been caring for him and observing him, looking for any sign that that traumatic damage his brain had done to itself was not absolute. Unfortunately, the message they were here to help us understand was one that had no hope. We knew what they were going to say, but inside I still held onto the desperate hope that any parent would in this situation; that they had discovered they were mistaken, and there was a brilliant loving child still there in that bed, just locked behind an injury that he would emerge from and eventually come back to us. But in the clearest way possible, they were here to make sure we understood that was not going to happen.

The lead doctor explained to us that the brain has several different pieces, but that the one place most important to life, the brain stem, the part of the brain that tells our bodies to breath when all other function is gone, had died on David. They had been monitoring his brain activity and there had been none. To me this was perhaps the cruelest irony of all. My son, who had possessed a brilliant mind full of lightning fast mathematical understanding and huge empathy, compassion and love, had ultimately lost the battle to survive because that same brilliant brain had for some reason sprung a leak and destroyed itself. The doctor explained that his eyes were unresponsive to light, there was no reaction to pain and nothing that would indicate activity was present. But to demonstrate the complete lack of brain activity he explained that they were going to disconnect the breathing machine. If there were anything still alive in his brain stem, when the oxygen level, measured by that little red light strapped to his finger, fell below a certain point, the most ancient and basic function that the brain stem had would kick in and the body would attempt to breath. Leslie and I nodded our agreement that we understood.

 I think in all transparent honesty, I have to admit something for those who may someday face this situation, or for those who have and are conflicted by the inner dialogue they are afraid to share with others; there were two major conflicting hopes going on inside of me. One of course, was that we would find some signal from David that he was still in there. But the other was one that may have been very selfish to a great degree, but was also geared toward the protection of my wife, my daughter, the lives we had built for ourselves, and the realities of what a small sign might mean. On some level I was hoping there would be no sign so this immediate nightmare of hospitals and doctors would be over and my boy could move on to wherever it is we all go. Truth is, I knew in my heart he had already gone there. I had spent enough time staring at him, talking to him, that I knew he was no longer in the room with us. A small sign of hope would only prolong this entire nightmare for days, months, years, or perhaps a lifetime. I'm not sure what kind of life that would have meant for us. Personally I can think of no more undesirable scenario than to be trapped behind a wall of silence, unable to use your body, or communicate, but simply laying there as the world happens around you, perhaps not even able to understand what transpired from minute to minute. I would not want that, and I did not want that for my beautiful boy. I didn't want that for Leslie, or for Abby. I am sure that if that had been the road we had been faced with, we would have done all we could to make the best of it, but it would have been a very difficult road. Losing David was proving to be devastating enough, but to lose him and yet have to care for him when he was unable to really live life, that to me was unimaginable.

So I stood there with Leslie as the doctor reached over and disconnected the breathing tube. For the next minute or so we watched as the oxygen level slowly declined. David's godfather was with us, and he was vocally urging David on to give us some kind of miniscule sign. The more he urged, the more I realized that was not what was going to happen, and secretly did not want to happen. Leslie and I have discussed this moment several times in the years since, and to my comfort and sanity, she was thinking the same thing I was. We both had already come to the realization that David was gone, and it actually made the moment that was unfolding more difficult to have someone urging on something that would only have brought more strife to everyone involved.

The oxygen levels dropped below the threshold, and the buzzer alarm sounded on his life support system. The nurse reached over and quickly shut it off. The doctor leaned in with his light and checked his eyes for any sign, but David lay there perfectly still. His body had no reaction to the impending end. There was no doubt left in anyone's mind; he was gone.

Knowing that we planned to donate David's organs so others could have life from our tragedy, the doctor reconnected the respirator, and the numbers started to slowly go up again. He looked at us with sad resignation, and Leslie and I nodded. He explained that the machines would keep his organs and body going for only so long, and that the longer he stayed on the machines, the more damage would be done to his organs, possibly making them unusable for transplant. We knew what this meant.

    We moved to another room and signed the paperwork that handed David over to One Legacy, the agency that would be handling the organ donation. She informed us that they would find matches for David's organs as quickly as possible and let us know when the time was to come that he would be removed from life support so they could "harvest the organs." I have to tell you, the phrase "harvest the organs" is perhaps the most unsavory phrase I have ever encountered in my life. It's completely accurate, but somehow is so incredibly cold and inhuman. I've tried to find a different combination of words that seemed less repugnant to me; "recycle," "salvage," "recover." They all have a certain air of indifference to them that does not do justice to what is actually happening. I like to think of it as David "sharing" his organs with someone else. It's a word he understood totally, and one that really describes the giving nature of the process, but sharing is something a person does willingly, and of course though I have no doubts it is what he would have wanted to do, he really had no say in the process.

    After all the signing Leslie and I went back to see him. The room was full of medical personnel, doing what they had to to ensure his organs would be in the best shape possible when he shared them. We asked, and were given, a few moments to be with him again, and then we left. It was our goodbye. We knew they would call us before the actual process of sharing took place, but neither Leslie nor I planned on coming back again. Our boy was gone. We had said our goodbyes. His body was now in the hands of people who were going to use it to save others. It was done.

    My father, who had not been dealing with the tragedy very well, had voiced his thoughts to my older brother that he thought we should all go back and see David again before the final procedure took place. I told my brother too tell him we'd play it by ear, that when we got the call it was imminent, we'd make that decision then. We were exhausted. We came home with our thoughts on planning a funeral. I started combing through our photo files on the computer, searching for the right pictures to do justice to David's all too short life. We watched some TV. We spent time with Abby. There was a peace that started to descend upon us to the extent that the unknown was over. We now knew what lay ahead, life without David.

Around 10 o'clock the phone rang. It was One Legacy. They wanted to tell us they had found matches for all of David's major organs, but there was a small complication involving the heart, and they wanted to know what we wanted to do. Apparently David's heart was a more difficult match to make for several reasons. There was no one in the United States that matched, and though they had found a match in Canada, it presented a problem. To make that connection work, due to time restrictions and other medical concerns, they would not be able to do the procedure for another day. That would put all the other organs in danger because David's body had already started breaking down. If we waited for the heart, odds were strong that the other organs might be unusable. Leslie and I consulted quickly and decided that helping more people was better, so we told them not to wait. They told us the procedure would begin within the hour, and if we wanted to see him one more time we should hurry. Leslie had no intention of going, we were both exhausted, and we felt confident we had said all we needed to. I called my brother and told him to tell my father what was happening. It was late, everyone was exhausted, and I told him I was not going back, there was no point.

That was it. After all the years of loving and caring and worrying about our first-born, it was over. We had made the decision to remove life support. He was gone. Even though I was spent both physically and emotionally, I sat up for several hours. I wanted to be awake as it all came to an end, even if I was not going to physically be in the room. Perhaps there was a part of me that thought he might show up in the dark corner of the room, glowing like Obiwan Kenobi at the end of RETURN OF THE JEDI, waving at me and giving me a his thumbs up. Perhaps I just wanted to be aware that I was alive and breathing. I slept well that night. I no longer had to worry about David. Now I had to worry about us. Where there once were four, only three remained.

TWO POEMS FROM A DARK PLACE

    After David died I wrote a few poems to try and get the scattered and broken feelings I had out into something that the writer and artist in me could make sense of. These two were the most effective in that regard. These are from the perspective of someone very recently thrust into a grief journey, a place of not having a clue as to what has just happened because a loved one has been senselessly ripped from their lives.

THE WELL

I knew the well was deep,
But I had no idea.

Until fate pushed me in,
I had no idea.

You are not at the bottom with me.
And the slick stones of grief are inescapable.

From a distant place of light I hear laughter,
but not yours.

The cold damp horror around me
threatens to swallow me whole.

Surely if you were here,
you would lower the rope,
as you did every day.

Your Laugh,
Your Smile,
Your Love.
Gone.

I fear that outside this solitary well,
People will forget.
Your Laugh,
Your Smile,
Your Love.

We had so much left to teach each other.
But I had no idea.

I miss you more than I could have ever thought possible,
But you have no idea…

EVERYWHERE

The family photos on the walls,
The closet full of toys in your room,
The sports trophies on the table,
How can I miss you so much,
when you're everywhere?

Your sister's smile,
Your mother's sobs,
Your empty bed,
How can I miss you so much,
when you're everywhere?

A crowd's triumphant cheer,
A baby's laugh,
A discarded "scratcher" lottery ticket on the ground,
How can I miss you so much,
when you're everywhere?

Every stranger's hug,
Every star in the night sky,
Every unanswered prayer,
How can I miss you so much,
when you're everywhere?

The hesitant "How are you?" from a friend,
The Hot Wheels Car on my office shelf,
The redundant music floating through the supermarket aisles,
How can I miss you so much,
when you're everywhere?

My loss of faith,
My shattered dreams,
My fondest memories,
How can I miss you so much,
when you're everywhere?

THE GROCERY STORE

In the days that immediately followed David's death perhaps there was nowhere more terrifying than the grocery store. The place I had spent countless shopping excursions begging my son and his little sister to stop running. Begging them to be polite and think of the other people in the store who were trying to shop and not to consider the store a playground. My son always got it and tried to rein his sister in, but she'd needle him a little, and before the second hand had gone full circle, they'd both be doing what I asked them not to. He knew I'd be annoyed, and it always made him feel bad, but they had a special bond these two. He was the protector, he knew what would make Leslie and I mad and what wouldn't, and most of the time he knew where the line they shouldn't cross was. I noticed in the days after his death, Abby had to learn where "the line" was. It wasn't where it used to be, and it was not where it would be in a month, 6 months, 1 year, or 5 years.

But those battles of wills and rules were the good memories of shopping. The truth was they were great kids, usually helpful, always full of life, even if they didn't always follow the rules, they knew them. We had taught them that.

No, the terror of the supermarket wasn't the memories so much; it was all those other people. The ones shopping who would make eye contact. Did they know? Did they know that one of the most special people in the world to me had been taken away? Did they know I was one fleeting memory away from flowing tears and crippling grief? Were they trying to put the face with the newspaper article they read, or were they one of the thousands at his vigil? Did their kid play football too, or had, or wanted to? Had they seen us around school? Church? The theater? Baseball? Softball? Work? Had they lost a child? A spouse? Parent? Sibling? Dog? Hamster? And when that tiny wave of recognition clicks on their face, what then? Were they going to say something? Oh God, I hoped they wouldn't say something, but if they had to, please make it short and sweet.

Or maybe worse yet, they didn't know. How dare them? How dare they stand there and not throw their arms out and wrap me up? No matter how much it made my skin crawl to hug someone again at that exact moment, how dare they not know, and not try? Didn't you read the newspaper? Watch the TV news? The greatest little boy that ever walked the face of this planet has died. My little boy. How dare they not know that!?!

And that was just the other customers. The employees all knew my son. He always said "Hi." He was one of those polite kids who came to the bakery, asked for a cookie, and said thank you when he got one. When I saw the lady in the bakery and she asked how I was I couldn't tell if she knew or not. I wanted to tell her. But I figured I was finally past the "Let me tell you what happened and make you feel bad because I really feel like dying and I can think of nothing I want more right now than to make you feel like dying too" stage. I just nodded and replied with "Hanging in there." She nodded.

Behind me though, I knew, only 20 feet from where I stood, was the sweet lady who worked in the pre-packaged meat and cheese aisle. She rotated the stock and gabbed with anyone who wanted to talk, and basically made shopping in this store a friendly experience. Over the years she had become a friend. She was very proud of her children. And she loved my kids. I had walked in the week before, knowing that she may not have heard. There in front of shiny packages of Oscar Meyer Bologna, and Ball Park Franks, she greeted me with her usual smile. I started to tear-up, realizing she hadn't heard. She sat down on the edge of the deli case and wept. Then she took my hand and we went outside and both wept. Again I was reminded that it wasn't just Leslie, Abby and I that had lost David. She came to the memorial. But every time I went back into that store, there she was stocking meats and cheeses. I'd pass, exchange a meaningful hand grasp, and move forward. There was nothing else to do.

As I'd continue through the store every face presented the same questions.

I started using a list, I had to, otherwise I would endlessly wander the aisles looking at everything I had ever bought, thinking of my son. "Tuna," he used to reach down and hand me the cans. Hot Pockets, he loved them for breakfast with his preference in taste leaning towards the sausage, not bacon. I'd see something he loved which we didn't usually buy, and into the cart it would go, I had to have one for him. Before I knew it I had a cart full of Cheetos, Garlic bread and Pringles.

So I'd get in line to check out. Which checker was on duty? Oh no, not the Manager. He had purchased the winning Football raffle ticket from my son last year. He had played on the same football field 30 years ago when he was growing up that my boy died on. He loved my boy. I couldn't face him again. He'd understand.

I would also avoid the checker with the weathered face and gentle eyes. She always asked about the kids and I didn't want to go through it again. I mean really, what was the appropriate thing to say to "Where are the kids today?" "Oh thanks for asking, my girl is in school, and my son is in an urn on top of the piano. How are you?"

I'd find a cashier on the end I didn't know. Longest line, but who cared. I'd punch in my member number (the Boy loved doing that for me). I'd open my wallet and absentmindedly pull out the credit card with the picture of the kids at the beach. My son was buried up to his neck in the sand, and his sister was grinning ear to ear, holding the shovel and pail. A great picture taken when we were camping that year. Inevitably the checker would notice.

Eventually, that credit card would start to bring a smile to my face, helping me remember the good times. But at first it was the last reminder on the way out of the store; the supermarket sucked.

ALLOWING OTHERS TO HELP

"You are never strong enough that you don't need help."
~Cesar Chavez
"When you're drowning, you don't say 'I would be incredibly pleased if someone would have the foresight to notice me drowning and come and help me,' you just scream."
~John Lennon

    I am no hero. But somewhere along the line in my life I developed the attitude that asking for help was a weakness somehow. Oh, I'm not talking about the little things like "Can you bring me a soda?" or "Can you reach the TV remote for me?" Abby will tell you I'm certainly lazy enough to ask for those things. No, I'm talking about big things. I was raised with a "don't bother people, do it yourself or go without" kind of attitude. And for much of my life it has served me well. In fact, in my chosen profession of actor and writer, it has been a great motivator to not get lazy, or ask for things from others, but to go out and make things happen. Perhaps it's a pride thing. As the youngest of 4 children, I always had a big brother or sister doing things for me, and was always desperate to be as big as they were. I would always shun the help being offered because I wanted to do it myself. So, when David died and my world crumbled around me my first instinct was not to look for help from those around me.

I'm not really sure who said it to me first, because I had multiple people tell me, in multiple different ways, before it sunk in.

"Let people help you."

This was a completely foreign concept to me.

"I don't need help."

"I can do it."

"I don't want to bother people."

"I'm strong, I can handle it."

Boy, was I a schmuck. Accepting help when you really need it is not weakness, though many feel it is. Being able to gracefully welcome those that see you hurting and are extending a hand to help is not easy, but it is a necessity if you are going to survive something like the loss of a child. It is in fact, strength of character to know when you are outside of your own abilities, and to seek aid. And the biggest realization I had that allowed me to accept help from others was that when you boil it down, by letting others help you, you are helping them.

One of the things Leslie and I became acutely aware of when David died was that we were not the only people who had lost a great deal and were in pain. From our best friend's wail on the phone when I told her he was gone, to his 10 and 11 year-old football teammates who cried when they spoke about him at the football field, there was a whole community that was grieving the loss of our son. David had worked his way into the hearts of everyone he met. These people needed to do something about it. They knew there was nothing they could do that would bring him back, but they felt compelled to do SOMETHING. Who were we to tell people, "No, this is our grief, and ours alone?" They all had different reasons for wanting to help. Maybe David had helped their kid with something at school, or they had admired his spirit and the determined way he ran laps at football practice. Perhaps they had a child that he reminded them of. Perhaps somewhere inside they felt guilty because they felt relief it was not their child who had died. It didn't matter why they wanted to help us, they felt compelled to do so, and let's be honest; we needed help.

I had to come to the realization that this help being offered was not on a quid pro quo basis. These people needed to reach out and help. Those meals that they wanted to bring in, and babysitting of Abby they offered came with no strings attached. The gifts they brought Abby weren't being brought because they were going to have a birthday party for their kid soon and wanted to make sure they were being reciprocal. No, these gifts of time and energy and things were pure and heartfelt sympathy.

It didn't take long to allow the help to come. Soon people were arranging details for the funeral for us, asking the local grocery store for donations of food and flowers for the service. People would bring food to the house, and when they did, they needed to talk with us, reach out personally and make sure we were going to be okay. It proved to be wonderful and gave Leslie and I the time we needed to do what we needed to do. I spent many hours preparing a video and music for his funeral. I needed to find the right songs and the right pictures that would sum up his life. We had to spend time with Abby to make sure she was finding her way forward through this nightmare. Being only seven years old, and suddenly having the house full of relatives and friends was very confusing for her. There were all these good things happening, people to play with, delicious foods, teddy bears and coloring books and all the attention. It's hard for anyone not to enjoy that. But she was also missing her brother, and seeing her mom and dad horribly sad. I remember about six months after David died talking with her to see how she was doing and sharing how sad it all made me. I said to her, "You probably never saw me cry before David's accident?" She let out a huge hearty laugh, "I NEVER saw you cry before." We both shared a laugh over that.

Interestingly, that was one of the others things having so many people offer to help allowed us, a chance to laugh. Part of healing is finding the good memories, sharing them with others and finding a way to laugh at them, and ourselves. I've always found a way to laugh at life and myself. After David died was no exception. Having the time and luxury to sit around and do nothing but dig through the memories we all had of him, and share stories with others that knew him was imperative in us starting to heal. Often it was hard to tell where the tears stopped and the laughter began, but that is only natural. It's amazing how much I learned about who David really was after he died. I heard stories of what he was like when we were not around. They made me proud. They made me miss him even more. They say you really don't know who your kids are until you get a chance to see them be themselves when you are not around. The stories I heard of things he had done reaffirmed that we had been in the company of a great little man, who had been taken not only from us, but from the world around him way too soon.

Allowing others to help was also a letting go. There was a relief of stress in just trusting that the little things would get done. What's that old saying, "Let go, and Let God?" Well there's a lot of truth in it. God is the people around you and the love they feel for you. God was present. He wasn't sitting in judgment or demanding dogma, he was coming to us in the people who had been in our lives and showing us that love is what matters.

Allowing others to help you when you most need it is a blessing, for yourself and for those that feel the need to help, for whatever reason. Let the help come. Everyone will be better for it. In accepting that help, you'll exhibit a strength that goes far beyond flesh and bone. Accepting that help was not just helping us, it was helping all those that loved and missed our boy.

I READ THE NEWS TODAY, OH BOY!

"Nothing travels faster than the speed of light with the possible exception of bad news, which obeys its own special laws."
~Douglas Adams

A bedroom community, like the one we lived in, where the world pretty much revolves around the children and families that reside there, doesn't generate a lot of news that is worthy of media vans with their satellite dishes unfurled high into the air very often. Even this close to Los Angeles, the need doesn't arise for those brightly painted rolling media studios to venture over the hillside on a regular basis. But when a 10-year-old buy with a bright smile and all-American face collapses at a practice for the country's favorite violent sport, they come like moths to the flame.

For the first 12 hours after David's accident we dealt with only the immediate situation at hand. But as time passed the following day the word spread like wildfire. That next morning at the hospital a group of my close friends, all with children of their own, converged on the hospital to see us. I met them down in the lobby not far from the garden where we had told Abby that her brother was not going to survive. There were tears and hugs, and the kind of support we were lucky to have around us that not everyone gets. It was good to see them and share our nightmare. Their presence helped.

About an hour after they left I got another call up in David's room. There was a group of people from the football league in the lobby inquiring about seeing us.

By now the word had spread like wildfire. The coaches, who had held vigil outside the hospital in Simi Valley the night before, had been told the bad news in person by me and were devastated. I'm sure they had shared the distressing news. I'm also pretty sure that the group down in the lobby the next day, the president of the league and much of the board that ran the league, were there for two reasons. The first was that they all had kids who played. Several of them had been at the field the night before, and they, like most people were in disbelief over what had happened and they needed to hear it themselves. They wanted to offer whatever support they could. The second reason they were there was, I'm sure, a much more practical reason. The league they were the shepherds of had been going strong in our town for over 45 years. Nothing like this had ever happened before. I am sure, and by no means do I hold this against them, they were concerned about what this would mean to them and the league legally. We hear about it all the time, someone dies, and the next thing that happens is lawyers get involved, and whether warranted or not, a huge lawsuit is filed and a small nonprofit league for kids is left to twist in the wind financially and does not survive. They were there on some level for damage control, and they were doing the right thing for the league.

What they heard from me was more shocking than they had anticipated. They came to the hospital hoping to offer prayers and plans for a vigil for David to get better the next night. Instead, they got the news from me that he was not going to survive. They were stunned. They asked if it was still okay to hold the vigil the next night at the field as a memorial for David. I of course told them yes. They said that if Leslie and I and Abby wanted to attend that would be great, but by all means if we could not they would understand, but they would like to do it anyway. I remember one question in particular: "The helmet he was wearing, was it one of ours?" I assured them that no, it was his, bought new this year to protect him. I'm pretty sure I saw an exchange of looks between a couple of them at that piece of news that had a bit of relief in it; good, no lawsuit there! They seemed relieved that I had so openly agreed to speak with them, and that there was no anger in me at that time aimed at the league or our coaches. Truth is, I never had any anger towards the league over David's accident. I was at practice with him every night. He had not been pushed too hard, or made to do dangerous exercises. He had been coached properly to play the game. Nothing that had happened on the field pointed to neglect. In fact, as time has passed, even though David died on the football field, practicing with his team and wearing a football uniform, his accident really wasn't the sport's fault.

They left that morning, being very conscientious of my time and need to be with David and my family. The President offered one last thought as they left, "We've already had a few calls from the media, but I want you to know we'll do everything we can to keep them at a distance."

"The Media."

I hadn't thought of that until right then.

I nodded, "Thank you. Yeah we don't want to talk to anybody."

They understood. In fact they were probably glad. If we came out of our shock at this accident and decided we were going to sue, not having the media involved was a good thing for them as well.

That evening as people descended on us, we received a few calls from the local media, but we politely told them we had no interest in speaking with them. The next day there was lots of activity around the house with relatives and people offering support. The league called again to let us know what time the rally would be happening, and to assure us that they had a parking spot nearby the main area for us so we would be inconvenienced as little as possible if we chose to attend. I told them it was our plan to be there, we knew that it was important for the kids to have a chance to share with us. They again mentioned that the media had made it clear they were going to be in attendance, but they had made arrangements to run interference so they would not get near us if we didn't want them to.

We spent time with David that afternoon, and went though the nightmare of seeing ourselves that our boy was truly gone. We went home to attend the memorial rally. I really hoped that the national media would not pick up this event. We were just at the beginning of the media's focus on injuries in football, and the last thing I wanted was for our boy to become some kind of poster boy for the cause. My brother, who has experience in crowd situations thanks to his job as a university VP helped organize the car caravan to the field. As we approached the field it became apparent that a lot of people were there. Cars were parked quite a distance from the field itself and lots of people, many of them in their football jerseys, and many from leagues outside our town, were walking towards the field. We drove down to the back gate and they motioned us right in. We pulled in behind the stands, and there waiting for us were David's teammates.

These boys were all between the ages of 10 and 12. I could see on their faces that they needed to see us. I had been their team manager so they all knew me very well from the sidelines and from practices. I'm proud to say we had a lot of respect for each other. This bunch of tough warriors all had tears running down their faces and when I went to them they came forward and hugged me en mass. I knew they needed to hear something. Standing right in the middle was the young man who had tackled David on the last play at that fateful practice. I knew that he, more than any of them, needed to hear something. Through tears, I told them that David loved them all, and that what had happened was no one's fault. I especially made that point to the one who truly needed to hear it. I told them that there was nothing in the world he enjoyed more than getting out there in his uniform with all of them and playing that game together. I told them that what had happened was a freak accident, and that he would want them all to know he did not blame them in any way. We all hugged again, and then Leslie and I made our way to our seats.

The football field where David had spoken his last words to me was full of parents and kids. Players in their uniforms and cheerleaders in theirs stood on the field holding candles and crying. It was Saturday, a day when normally there would still be a late game playing on this field, but the league within our town, and the entire regional league we played in, had canceled games that day out of respect for what had happened. There were over 2500 people gathered here to pay tribute to David. Many of them had never known him. It was humbling to see the outpouring of love for our boy.

Over the course of the next hour or so coaches stepped forward and talked about our boy. They regaled the crowd with stories of the little guy who cried as he ran laps at the field, but never stopped. They spoke of David as an inspiration who wanted nothing more than to give all he had to contribute to his team. They called him "Coach" and explained how this smart young man, with a keen sense of the game and how it should be played, would write up plays for the team in his notebook.

After the coaches, the most amazing thing happened. One by one, every single one of his teammates stepped up to the microphone. These were young men, most of whom had never stood at a microphone, let alone in front of a sea of people and TV cameras. They spoke of David. Each of them had something to say. They spoke of how David never gave up or stopped trying. They spoke of how David never got mad at anyone. They spoke of how he was always kind and supportive and most of all enthusiastically a true teammate. A few, including the young man who I know blamed himself for this, spoke about how, when they first met him three years earlier, weren't sure David was going to make it in football, but that David had taught them to never give up, because David had worked so hard he was now a starter on the team. They spoke of how they loved him. These were boys of 10, 11 and 12, being open and honest about their pain and heartache. It was inspiring to Leslie and I, and made us so very proud of our son.

At one point a father stepped forward who had not been given permission to speak. He went on and on about David and me, and how supportive we had been to his son who had not been able to make the team due to his weight. He was the only man who spoke that night that made me angry. He had been an assistant coach before his son had been cut, and the parents did not like him. He was harsh and represented the things we did not want around our boys. He had shamed David in one practice for wearing extra forearm pads to protect himself from being hurt. Quite simply, this guy was an asshole. I had told the head coach that earlier in the year, and we all had breathed a sigh of relief when his son had been cut so that we didn't have to deal with him anymore as a coach. The fact he felt he had a right to step forward, and speak about my boy infuriated me, but thankfully those in charge knew to remove him as quickly as possible from the microphone.

Finally, the head of the league read a message Leslie and I had written that we asked him to read. It's ironic, even though I have spent my entire life getting on stage and trying to get attention; at that moment I had no interest in being up in front of the crowd. After the reading, everyone was instructed to light their candles and take one more lap in David's honor around the field. They played the Greenday song "Good Riddance (Time Of Your Life)" which ironically was the only song David ever really loved. It's a song that was written by Billy Joe Armstrong after his father had died, and includes the lyric: *"It's something unpredictable, but in the end is right, I hope you had the time of your life."*

Mercifully the TV trucks had been kept at a respectable distance. After the lap, a chant of "David" emerged from the gathered mass and we gravitated to the center of the field with his team. It was only then that someone from the media got to us. She had a microphone at her side and introduced herself quickly. A few people attempted to step in but I turned rather harshly towards her and barked, "Are you kidding me?" But she quickly put her hands up and explained, "I don't want to intrude, I just wanted you to know, someone in my family was the recipient of an organ donation last year, and I think it's a beautiful thing you did donating his organs. Thank you." I nodded thanks, and she turned and left, respecting our privacy. It was actually a beautiful thing to share with us.

  That night David was the top story on every local news channel. They all covered the story respectfully, but all noted that the exact cause of death had not yet been released. This of course meant that the story was not over.

  It was two days later when the Los Angeles Coroner's office decided to release the results of David's autopsy without informing us first. Things started popping up online about cause of death being an acute head injury. We started getting messages and emails about it. Now we already knew this, but reporters were starting to chime in about how it was a head injury, and apparently many of them decided to ignore the term "acute." An "acute" injury is one that happens suddenly. It is not a lingering injury, or one that is the result of repeated injury over time. Many of the online and newspaper reports got that wrong, or ignored it, and instead waxed poetic about how undiagnosed or untreated injuries can lead to head trauma that becomes deadly. This was not the case with David. It was hurtful to read people that did not know us and did not know the situation making it sound as if his family or team had been negligent and that was what had led to David's death. I called the LA Coroner's office the next day and ranted at whoever would listen about how irresponsible it was to release the autopsy information to the media before releasing it to the family. They apologized profusely, but in the same breath informed me the information was public record and the news organizations were waiting to find out what had caused David's death. Thankfully, again, the story did not go further into the mainstream media, and we were not tortured with the misinformation for long.

A week or so later I got a call from the LA County Coroner's office, and they apologized again for the confusion in releasing the information. They also wanted to specifically reassure me and Leslie that after a special consultation between all the doctors involved, including the neurosurgeon who had done the original emergency surgery, it was their conclusion that what happened to David was a freak occurrence. They saw no reason to assume that his injury had been something we had missed. They were honestly trying to put or minds at ease that we had done nothing that contributed to his death. It was appreciated.

One more note here about the media, and now I speak not of the organized media avenues of reporters and journalists, but of the Wild West of the media known as the internet. Let me first say that I knew better than to do what I did, but curiosity got the best of me. After some of the less accurate reports of his cause of death came out I was foolish enough to read comments left online about the articles. OH MY GOD! There is a safety and freedom people feel online that they obviously don't entertain in face-to-face contact. People who had no idea of what they were talking about vilified our family in the comments sections. Half of the posters used our tragedy to spout off about bad irresponsible parenting, bad coaching, the dangers of football and just about anything else you can imagine. In fairness, many of the other comments attempted to get people to think twice before they typed such hateful things because heaven forbid someone from the poor boy's family, like me, would be reading the comments. This of course prompted more vilification for not being off grieving about my son but for being online and reading what people were saying. It was a low point in observing humankind for me.

Thankfully I have a thick skin, and a logical mind that only let the rabid displays of human nature run amuck affect me a little bit. But I stopped looking at the comments very quickly. The last contact we had with the media was just before his funeral services later in the week. The local newspaper called and asked permission to attend and cover his funeral. I denied their request. I told them that we had specifically not spoken to the media because David's accident was not something we wanted sensationalized. They understood and thanked me for my time.

A couple of months later, two young ladies at the two local high schools organized a touch football game between their cheerleading squads and decided to raise funds with it for David's memorial fund. I didn't know the girls, but they had been moved by his story, and they wanted to do something to help. We were very touched. At this time we decided to do an interview with local TV to thank the young people involved and to thank our town of Simi Valley for all they had done for us during this nightmare. The interview was going to be on our terms and there would be no scenes of us wailing or crying uncontrollably. We simply took the opportunity to thank the town and the cheerleaders for their contributions to David's memorial fund and talk about what a great place our town was. It was a nice piece that we felt accomplished the goal of saying thanks publicly to as many people as we could.

Overall, considering the potential for David's story to have been sensationalized, we were fortunate in how the media treated us. It very well could have spun out of control in several different ways and left us feeling used and battered. Thankfully we also had no one to lash out at and no reason to take the story to the media for those kinds of purposes. I'm not passing judgment on anyone that embraces the media for whatever purpose, but for my family and me, I think it respected David not to let it become a spectacle. I didn't need to prove to the world how much pain we were in. Those close to us, and the whole town seemed to know and understand. I believe it helped our family not to turn our pain into TV theatrics. It allowed us to focus on our love, our loss, and our family. But make no mistake, the media was there, ever hungry to jump on the story and trot out personal tragedy for the sake of ratings. Thank goodness we did not take the bait.

THE VIEWING & FUNERAL

To those outside the immediate circle of loss, the funeral is the end of the process. Of course we all know that it's the time after the funeral that is the most challenging for those that are grieving. But the funeral is the big public goodbye. It's the time for those who are close and not so close, to have that moment to say goodbye, and to tell those that are left behind how sorry they are for the loss. After David's funeral I couldn't help but think it was all very much like a big Anti-Wedding.

I spent hours putting together pictures and music I thought was appropriate. After I had a list, Leslie and I went over it and over it. It wasn't just the funeral, but there was going to be a viewing as well. We sat together in my office and played songs. Some were familiar songs that we knew others would identify with and would find appropriate for the occasion. Others were songs that meant something to us. The test was if we both felt the song was okay to have, or if one of us really wanted it and the other didn't have a big objection to it, we'd include it.

I was thankful that when it came time to deal with a funeral parlor my big brother was there. He had worked many years ago for a family friend who ran a funeral home, and he was familiar with many of the issues we were going to have to deal with. The biggest problem was going to be making sure we had David in time for the viewing and service. The coroner's office had wanted to examine David, as was normal under the circumstances of his death. But apparently there was a bit of a death back up at the LA County coroner's office, and they could not guarantee that they would be able to release the body in time for our planned services. Thankfully our funeral home had a good relationship with them, and they were able to expedite the process. I don't know what that involved, and don't really care, but David was not late to his own funeral. The other thing that was troublesome was the warning several people involved in the process felt the need to keep repeating. Without getting into gory details, we were informed that often when a person is kept on life support for a few days in order to maintain the organs so they could be donated to those in need, the body often can suffer changes that make it difficult to have a viewing where the dead look anything like they did in life. The funeral director assured us his mortician was very skilled and would do the very best he could to make sure our boy looked like our boy. It did not put two grieving parents who were already at the end of their rope at ease. I had horrible thoughts of arriving at the viewing and having David looking nothing like David. It was agreed that on the night of the viewing we would arrive a bit earlier so that we could spend a little time with him in private, and also, if he was not presentable, close the coffin and simply have a large picture of him on an easel next to the casket.

  So the night came for the viewing, and we caravanned over to the funeral parlor. As we arrived the funeral director greeted us and assured us that he felt the mortician had done a very nice job with David. We were led into the viewing area, and there he was. My son was lying in a coffin. He wore his USC hat, one of his favorites, which helped hide the top of his head where emergency surgery had been done. He looked like David. He wore the "Stop Homework" graphic t-shirt he loved so dearly. Leslie and I had decided that his final outfit should be totally him. Neither of us felt it was proper to dress him in a suit or tie, that was not our boy. The coffin he was in was a "display" coffin. Since he was going to be cremated we had forgone purchasing a coffin and were simply renting this one. That was just another of the odd choices we got to make in this whole process. In the adjoining room there was food that had been arranged by our dear friend that lived behind us. She had gone to the local supermarket, and they had donated cookies and ice cream. They knew us and David's tragic tale was all over the news. The music I had put together played over the speakers. It's funny, I had several people compliment me on the musical choices I made. A strange comment at a time like this, but people didn't know what to say, so they were saying anything positive they could think of.

    That evening is very much a blur to me now. But there are a few moments that are burned into my memory. One was of a father and his two sons, who were from a neighboring town. They arrived at the viewing wearing their football jerseys. They had never met David, and they knew nothing of the special young man he was to all of us, but they felt compelled to be here. They were part of the family that was football. This father knew the risks that were involved, and he wanted his sons to understand, that even though they didn't know him personally, they had a connection through the sport they loved and David died playing. They were grieving for him. This same response came from several places in the football world. Even as high up as the NFL's Minnesota Vikings. We received a check for David's memorial fund from the then head coach of the Vikings, Brad Childress. By some strange twist of fate, his mother lived in our little town. When she told him of David's death while practicing for a team called the "Vikings" Mr. Childress was moved to send a check of $1000 to David's fund. I've never met him, and he's never met us, but it was the brotherhood of football that connected us. I sent him a thank you note, and included in it a few of the plays David had been diagramming for his football team. I told him that David had been nicknamed "coach" by his team, and that these plays, though surely simplistic compared to NFL play calling, might just be what he needed to pull out some day to help the "real" Vikings win. Of course I never heard back from him. But in my mind, Mr. Childress looked those plays over and perhaps gleaned some kind of inspiration in David's diagrams. You never know.

Other moments that struck me so powerfully and have stayed with me were two distinctly different parents who shared with me their stories of losing a child. Both of these people I had encountered during my years in this town, one through sports, and one at our church. To be honest, I'm not sure I could honestly tell you I liked either of them very much. They weren't bad people by any means, but our personalities had never really meshed. After David's death both approached me during the viewing. One told me how they had lost a young daughter a few years back. He told me he understood everything I was feeling. He suggested Compassionate Friends to me. He told me that if there was ever anything I needed, even just someone to yell and scream at and cry with, he would gladly be there. Of all the people that offered up this kind of blanket offer of support, his was one that I felt was truly sincere. I could see in his eyes he knew. He had been where I was. He understood. If I needed him I knew that there would never be any judgment from him, just an ear to listen. The other was an older couple from our church. I had always seen them as a bit distant and aloof to those around them. You might even describe them as snooty. As she approached me at the viewing there was a part of me that dreaded having to talk with her. I had a feeling of resentment that she was there; after all we really were not close in any way. But when she took my hand, hers was trembling. She looked at me and started to speak, Tears welled in her eyes. Through a strained and quivering voice she told me that she and her husband had lost their only son years ago. She told me that ever since she had been protecting her heart and emotions because most people could never understand. Suddenly everything I had ever experienced interacting with this woman made sense. She was aloof and a bit standoffish. She had to be, because even now, years later, when she let her guard down, she was devastated. She was still grieving and wounded, and the loss of her child had never healed. We shared a warm embrace, and again, I understood. From that day on whenever we saw each other, we exchanged a knowing glance. She never lost control of her emotions again, but several times told me how glad she was to see me, and how glad she was to see we were continuing to live our lives as fully as possible. I believe she lost a piece of herself when her son died that she was never able to regain, and that her wound was very deep. None of us ever get over the loss of our child, but some move forward with more assurance and healing than others. Though she had been able to continue with her life, her loss took a large toll on her.

    I also spent some time with David's favorite coach, the one that would yell "Butt up Sumner!" from the sidelines during games. I had asked, and he had agreed to speak at David's funeral. During the funeral he lead the boys on the team, who all wore their football jerseys, in a short call and response to honor David. But the night of the viewing he was struggling with what had happened. He had shared to a few around the team that he was through with coaching. After years and years of guiding young men and shaping them through football, he had decided this was the end and he could not go forward. I sought him out that night, and though my boy laid in his casket no more than forty feet from us, I reminded him of all he had given to David. He had given David confidence to be strong and keep working. He had shown David true respect and had given him humor and friendship that had gone beyond just a coach and player. He and David had formed a true friendship. He was David's favorite, as he was for most of the team. I reminded him how much David had cherished him. And I assured him that Leslie and I cherished him as well. I believe I said "Don't you dare stop sharing your knowledge and support to these young men because of this." We both had tears rolling down our faces, but I wanted him to know that what I saw him give these boys every time they stepped on the field was not only a blueprint to be successful football players, but also what it took to be a man. Strong, playful, self-deprecating and proud to be who they were. He was coaching football, but he was teaching boys to become well-rounded respectful men, and he could not let a senseless tragedy stop that. He understood, and took what I said to heart. He got back to coaching the boys for the rest of the season, but he was never quite the same. He had recently become a grandfather, and after David's death, he turned his attention to loving those kids. I have since lost contact with him. I believe he had trouble forgiving himself for what had happened even though we assured him it was not his fault. For some people, seeing us was too difficult after David died.

  The day of the funeral is also a bit of a blur. I know that the church was overflowing with people. A dear friend of Leslie's sang for us, a John Denver song, "Perhaps Love." He's a professional singer and he sang beautifully, but on the last verse he made the mistake of looking down at our family, and when he made eye contact with Leslie, he had trouble holding it together.

  Four people spoke. One was David's godfather, who had been with us when the final decision to remove life support had been made. He spoke of how David had been a better more loving person than he has ever been. David's favorite teacher spoke too, regaling us with tales of David's fierce hunger to learn and explore numbers and his endless curiosity and kindness to others. As I mentioned earlier, David's favorite coach spoke as well, including David's teammates in his words, and spinning stories of David's individual determination and drive to be not just the best football player, but also the best David that he could be. The final speaker was David's oldest cousin. She had spent a summer with us a few years earlier, and she and David had forged a very close relationship. Two years before he died, she had asked David to speak at her wedding. And even though David was only 8 and not a big fan of speaking in front of people, he wanted to do it for her. It had been a very special day for him. She spoke about the things David had taught her. She said he had taught her the delight of being a kid by playing game after game with her the summer she spent with us. She said he also taught her the importance of being a grown-up, and that even at the age of four his nature and countenance spoke of the importance of being kind and caring to others. She spoke of the time she had spent with our family, and how the love we shared was something she hoped to have someday in her own family. She spoke of how he taught her the importance of love, and how she could only hope to have a son as special as he was some day. But what she said that has stayed with me the most and helped me move forward through the grief was a quote she shared from Christopher Robin to Winnie the Pooh, "If ever there is tomorrow when we're not together there is something you must always remember. You are braver than you believe, stronger than you seem, and smarter than you think. But the most important thing is, even if we're apart, I'll always be with you." She and Christopher Robin were right; David has always been with me.

There was a video of pictures of David's life that played, which even though I had put it together, had me crying the whole way. Our pastor, who had been with us in the hospital the night of his accident, offered up some comforting words. And then it was over.

Our neighbor had arranged to have ice cream in an adjoining building where the kids and adults could make their own sundaes, something David would have loved. I hear it was wonderful, but Leslie and I never got to the ice cream room, because after the funeral we stood in front of the church and hugged and kissed hundreds who had to say hello and offer their condolences. The long line of people choking back tears, desperate to make sure they held us for a few moments, made the reception line at our wedding seem puny.

It was exhausting. It was cathartic. And when it was over I was ready to crawl into a hole and disappear.

It did David proud.

LAST TIME THROUGH THE DRIVE-THRU

The fast food drive-thru is one of those uniquely American places. It was born out of the American love of the automobile and it's freedom. Yes, we're so free and independent we can have people from inside a little window hand us our food so we can drive away eating our supersized fries without being bothered by anyone or anything. Free to listen to Barry Manilow as loud as we please without anyone looking at us funny as we spill special sauce down our fronts while belting out 'Looks Like We Made It' at the top of our lungs. Well, much to my surprise this bastion of freedom and independence proved not to be so wonderful on a couple of occasions after David had died.

It was a few days after David's funeral service and I was home in my office. I was seated in front of my MAC mindlessly playing video games trying to keep my mind from wandering back to images of David lying in his coffin. The family had all gone home, and I was into perhaps the hardest part of the grief journey; being left alone with myself for the first time. There were plenty of things I could do, but they all would remind me of David, and I was in prime avoidance mode at the moment. When the phone rang it startled me from my video poker inspired stupor and I answered it. It was the funeral parlor; "David" was ready to be picked up.

We had chosen to have David cremated and his ashes were now waiting. Oh joy. On the bright side it was something to do, and one of the last steps in this nightmare. And there was a part of me that was curious. I had never held an urn, or seen someone's ashes in person. I'd seen tons of movies and sitcoms that always seemed to think it was just hilarious to show people accidentally spilling someone's ashes everywhere, or worse yet having them end up in someone's coffee or the like. I got in my SUV and headed to pick my son up one last time.

I walked into the funeral parlor but there was another viewing going on in the rear, so I unobtrusively made my way into the office and told them I was here to pick up my son. I had phrased it just like that "To pick up my son," thinking it might be ironically humorous, but the stone-faced lady behind the desk had obviously become numb to attempts at witty death humor, and just pointed to the table next to the window. There, a large purple velvet bag concealed his urn. It had a nice little purple rope cord tie at the top. I couldn't help but think the whole thing looked like some large over sized, oddly shaped Crown Royal commercial. The size of it surprised me. We had selected a round polished stone urn from the catalogue, short and squat, and I hadn't realized how large it actually was. I opened the top of the velvet bag just enough to see that it was indeed the grayish stone we had ordered. I pulled the rope ties closed. I attempted to pick it up. It was *really* heavy. The velvet material of the bag slid against the round polished stone urn inside and damned if in the first 3 seconds of holding my son's ashes it didn't nearly slip out of my hands and crash to the floor, and do exactly what I had seen done in all those sitcoms.

"Careful it's heavy," offered "Morticia" behind the desk.

"Thanks."

I repositioned my hands, carefully lifted it up and cradled it in my arms. I thanked "Mrs. Adams" and headed out the door. As the front door to the funeral parlor closed behind me, tears came to my eyes and I whispered softly, "Come on pal, let's go home."

I got to the car and jokingly said to the urn, "Come on, you can ride up front with me." Of course this was something I had never let David do while he was alive. All those stickers on the sun visors of the car warned against letting smaller children ride up front because of the airbag dangers and the possibility of "serious injury or death," but since we had already covered that scenario I figured what the hell, we'll give him a thrill. After placing him on the passenger seat I climbed in and buckled up. The biting irony and sarcasm was strong with me that day and I jokingly thought, "Make sure you buckle up pal." But then it dawned on me, leaving him on the seat might not be a good idea. If I had to stop suddenly that round little rock like urn would very easily roll forward off the seat and I'd find myself home in ten minutes using the dust-buster to get him out of the car. I thought for a moment about putting the seatbelt around him, and then realized I was going down the crazy trail. I took hold of the urn and lowered it down onto the floor of the passenger compartment.

As I pulled out of the parking lot my stomach growled. I realized I hadn't eaten anything all morning. But hey, there was a McDonald's right around the corner. Again sarcasm stepped up and I found myself joking to myself that David would get a kick out of going through the drive-thru, he loved McDonalds. So I turned on the radio and pulled into line to order some food. I had just gotten to the point of no return, where the curb had me locked into line when I noticed it.

David's football team had gotten stickers made for the team to put on their helmets as a tribute to David. It was David's number "18," inside a little football. They had given us a roll of them and unbeknownst to me, parents had started putting them on their cars in addition to adorning the boys' helmets with them. There, on the rear window of the SUV in front of us, was one of these stickers. It wasn't rational in any sense of the word the gut reaction that swept through my body at that instant. First, it was like a punch in the face. Even though on the floor next to me was my son's urn, seeing his number on the car, the first time I had seen one of these stickers on a car, was an immediate shock and my mind was flooded with emotion. Instantly the shock turned to anger. I was furious for a few seconds that whoever the hell it was in front of me had the audacity to put my son's number, DAVID'S NUMBER, on their car like some stupid stick figure family! I'm pretty sure I even yelled inside the car, "Who the F*ck do you think you are?" Then the tears poured down my face as I realized it was probably someone from his team, and they were just trying to pay tribute to my boy and deal with his accident themselves. Suddenly I was gripped with fear. Had they seen my outburst? Was that a parent I knew driving the SUV? I quickly scanned the rearview and side view mirrors to see if they were looking at me or if I could make out who it was. I couldn't tell, but they certainly weren't looking at me, so at least that was good. I let them pull up and didn't pull up directly behind them. Mercifully they got their food quickly and were gone.

    I was drained emotionally. I got my food and drove home.

    I carried David into the kitchen counter and placed him down on the counter. I undid the rope ties and slid the velvet bag down completely for the first time. I carefully lifted the urn and slid the bag off. It was then I realized that David's urn was smiling at me. I kid you not. The stone used to make the urn had obviously been pieced together, a few different pieces layered to create the 8 inch high vessel. I'm sure most times this is done so the seams are practically unperceivable. But apparently whoever put David's together either didn't notice or didn't care that the different pieces of stone had markedly different shades of grey. The result was what looked like a giant smile across the front of the urn. I laughed. I'm sure the majority of folks who would have uncovered this urn would have found it completely unacceptable, but it made perfect sense to me. I loved it. I wasn't sure if Leslie would feel the same, but it worked for me. As it turns out, it struck Leslie the same way it struck me; David was smiling for us. In fact it was so perfect that we put one of his old baseball hats on the top. The hat fit perfectly, and though many of you might find this a bit macabre, it has been on that smiling urn ever since.

There was another time about a week later Leslie and I stopped to get some fast food on the way home. Neither of us were dealing with the world very well that day so we decided to use the drive-thru so as not to have to talk to anyone. Sure enough, just as we reached the point of no escape, the driver's door of the car in front of us swung open. Out popped one of the Dads from David's baseball team. He had not been in town when David had passed and he just had to get out of the car and come give us his regards. Of course it was sweet and we appreciated the gesture, but we were trapped and had no escape. He stood and talked with us longer than either of us wanted. We had both had a draining day, and we really didn't want to rehash it all at that particular moment. But he needed to express his thoughts and sadness for us. I know it sounds petty and small of us, but we wanted to be anywhere but there listening to him express his sympathy. We'd had had our fill. But, we were both polite and patient. Thankfully he eventually he got back in his car. It wasn't his fault. But neither of us needed that.

I was more cautious for the next couple of months pulling into drive-thrus. I'd like to say I ignored them, but grabbing greasy food became a habit I used to feed the grief. But it's rare I pull into a drive-thru that those two incidents don't run through my head to this day, and remind me that my boy died.

BUT HE DOESN'T KNOW ANYBODY

Each individual religion has its own unique vision of what the afterlife looks like. Many follow the rough idea that after death you travel to a place that is inhabited by all the wonderful souls that have passed before awaiting your arrival on the other side to greet you and welcome you to paradise. The common way of thinking is that there is a bright light down a long tunnel that beckons you forward, emerging into a bright place filled with glorious mist and wonderment.

It was this vision that a short time after David died brought great fear and angst to me. As I have already admitted, I was not before and certainly have not since been a religious man. But, I was raised going to church occasionally and the common culture there paints the aforementioned idyllic picture of an afterlife. And in the immediate tumultuously emotional wake of David's death I was grasping at straws, looking for anything to help make sense of this senseless tragedy. So thoughts of everything anyone had ever said to me about death was filtered through my pain as I grasped for something positive to hold onto.

Of course the idea that he had moved on to paradise was an obvious thought, but no sooner had the miniscule comfort of him being in paradise flashed across my brain that a horrible thought occurred to me that made it exponentially worse. I realized that when my boy emerged into the light at the end of the mythical tunnel to Heaven there would be no one he knew there waiting for him. My dear 10-year-old boy had never known anyone that had passed on. Both sets of grandparents were still alive. No teachers or mentors had passed. Thankfully no siblings, or cousins or classmates had passed. Not even a family dog or cat had passed in his 10 short years. I went so far in grasping for someone he might know that it occurred to me there may be a few fish he had fed that were there, but that would not be a great deal of comfort. No, in my eyes this demure little man, who always preferred to step back and get the feel of a situation before joining in would arrive in paradise not knowing anyone. No one would be there to show him around. He would be alone. This thought devastated me.

Now I know those of you with strong religious beliefs would assure me that God, or Jesus, or whatever deity you believe in would be there to greet him and that that would be a wondrous thing for him. But the only thing I could see was that my boy, the one who got anxious and nervous in strange situations, would not have Leslie or I there for him to hold hands with. Heck, even if Abby were there with him he could play the brave big brother and be her guide, but that (Thankfully) was not the case. We had worked so very hard making sure David and Abby both felt safe and secure in their lives. I used to proudly recount to people that when we had moved from one house to another, and they were both very young and still taking afternoon naps, that they both had been so secure in their lives that even though a work crew was using jackhammers to tear down the old chimney in our new home, they both went to their beds for naps and slept without hesitation while the walls of their new home shook from the demolition. The irony of that cuts so very deep now, knowing that not only did we fail to keep David safe, but that Abby will live the rest of her life with a deep seated realization that though her life has the illusion of safety, she secretly knows that security can be shredded at any moment with one tragic turn of events.

There were moments in that mind numbing anguish where I fantasized that it would be better for him if I were with him. That perhaps the best thing would be for me to travel that long tunnel and join him, so he would not be alone. Then he and I would be able to explore his new journey, as we had the woods of the Sequoia National Forrest, potty training, the first day of baseball practice, or so many of the other things I had guided him through as he grew. Of course, I knew that was not an option. My place was here with his mother and sister. Our journey was to find a way forward through this nightmare together without him. Where he was, wherever that may be, it was his journey to take alone. I certainly never seriously considered taking my own life, but I would be dishonest if I said the thought did not cross my mind, at least fleetingly.

That brings me to one last thought on the subject of the afterlife. I no longer am afraid to die. Don't misunderstand me, I am in no hurry, and in the years that have passed since David's death, the hunger to live life has returned fully and I intend to delay the journey he has already taken for as long as possible. But the idea of death no longer scares me. I admit the concept is still one that as a human I cannot wrap my head around. My logical and practical mind knows what death is, at least in the most basic scientific terms. It means that everything stops. The body stops breathing, the mind stops working and as far as I can tell, it's over. That's what I saw with my boy and have seen with others who have died. Of course the seemingly obvious facts and the acceptance of those facts are two totally different things. The entire reason humans have a concept of an afterlife, and I am not stating one does not exist, is because we can cannot conceive of the world continuing to spin and life going forward for everyone but us. I am just like the rest of you. That seems impossible to me. There must be something on the other side. It is similar to the argument I have heard used for the reasoning that the Universe is infinite; "If the universe ends, then what's on the other side?"

It's a concept that as finite individuals we are incapable of comprehending. That's why, whether there is an afterlife or not, since we do not know, we come to a belief that there must be something. I guess you can count me as a hopeful nonbeliever. There is nothing in this world that I feel I know that I hope to be mistaken of more.

The point is that I have come to terms with not knowing. In eastern philosophies it is said there is no belief. A wise man knows what he knows, and accepts there are things he does not know, but he has no "Beliefs." I have become very comfortable with that ideal. When it comes to the concept of death I have decided there are two possibilities. Either I will cross over in some way to the next adventure, in which case I have no doubt David will be there laughing and grinning and waiting to show me the wonders that await, or there will be nothing. If there is nothing, I won't know it, and there will be no disappointment, no regret, and no realization of having been right or wrong on the issue. But if there is another chapter, be it Valhalla, Heaven or whatever you may choose to call it, I will gladly eat crow and be thankful that my mortal incarnation was wrong. It certainly won't be the first time, just the last.

Until that day comes, I will move forward with my life as if there is no next chapter. I will live my life for the here and now, and try as best as I can to leave something of value behind that will last into the future even though I may not. And if nothing tangible is left behind, then perhaps the fact that, while I was here, I tried to spread joy and laughter to others through my life's work in the entertainment field will count for something. Hopefully, I will have the opportunity to help many more through Healing Improv, the nonprofit I have started where I put the improv games and structures I know so well to use in workshops helping others struggling with grief. David would like that, because in a very real way, it is his legacy that created it and is giving aid to others. If you think about that the right way, then he is not alone wherever he is, but rather he takes with him the good karma and blessings of the smiles and comfort of the work he inspired, and the love of people he does not know, but who know him through these pages and our workshops.

SPEAK HIS NAME, PLEASE

> *"I mean, they say you die twice. One time when you stop breathing and a second time, a bit later on, when somebody says your name for the last time."*
> ~Bansky

When a person you love dearly dies, one of the hardest things to come to terms with is the reality you will never see them again, you will never hear their laughter, you will never hug them, or feel their touch, or smell them or simply enjoy the presence of them being there beside you watching the idiot box silently from the couch. All interaction is gone. The only place they live on is in your memory. The good things cement themselves in your reminiscences forever and much of the bad or annoying things fade away. The fact that there are no new memories to be made is oft times crippling. Because of this, tears and weeping happen at the drop of a hat. And let's face it, most people are uncomfortable when someone they are talking to suddenly becomes misty eyed, and their voice begins to tremble. Perhaps this is why most people are afraid to mention the person that died in conversation. The trepidation of bringing the griever pain and heartache keeps people from discussing them at all.

I suppose this is very natural. When we see someone who is devastated by something, the last thing we want to do is pile on more pain. Often you hear the phrase, "I didn't want to mention (Insert dead person) because it might make (Insert griever) sad." Let me clue you in; WE ARE ALREADY SAD!

We have not forgotten. I have not gone forward in my life and magically forgotten my son died four years ago. There is no moment in my life since then that the memory of watching my son's eyes close, never to open again, has faded from my thoughts. It is with me every second of every hour. When good things happen in my life I think of David and how he would have loved it. When bad things happen in my life, I think of David and I'm thankful he didn't have to be there for those times. When I'm bored, I wish he were there because he could entertain me. When I eat good food, I think how he would have liked it. When I fart, I think of the noise he used to make on his arm and how we would laugh. He is never more than the tiniest step away from being there in my memory. But because I grieved, and cried for hours on end, I have learned to deal with that sadness, and it has become a part of me. And one of the most important parts of that grieving was talking about him endlessly after he died.

I know that after her brother died, Abby tread very carefully around the subject of her brother. She had never seen Leslie and I so devastated and depressed and I'm sure that it not only hurt her, but scared her. If we had let her, I imagine she would have buried most of her feelings in fear that talking about David would bring us too much pain and heartache. Because we knew this, we talked about our feelings all the time. Everything I went through was a chance to discuss my feelings with Abby so she knew why I was so sad and that it would be damaging not to be sad over what had happened. We told stories about David, and I shared the hopes and dreams that had been stolen from me, so she would understand that those feelings of being cheated were normal and healthy. Often it led to tears on my part, but I told her that the tears were welcome. If there were no tears there would be no healing. I'm not sure at 7 years of ages she completely understood, but she didn't need to understand, the message got through. Crying was Good. Crying was natural. Every tear honored David and kept us tied together as a family, and kept him near us. She got it. She still would hesitate sometimes to bring him up, and when she eventually did, I could see her watching us, judging our reactions and looking to see if what we were saying about the tears being good was true.

But for other people in our life, this has not always been the case. People have, and still do, avoid mentioning his name to us. I'm sure it's because they fear upsetting us. But I think it's something more than that too. I think it's because people are afraid themselves to tread back into that nightmare. Leslie and Abby and I have lived the nightmare of losing David every single moment of every day he has been gone. If I want to, I can find the tears over it in a moment. But to be able to move forward, we have cried hard and long, and for us, the day to day has returned to normal. The pain is with us always, but we have faced it, looked it squarely in the eye and come to understand and accept it. Other people seem to be more like the wizards and witches in the Harry Potter book series who were afraid to mention Voldemorte's name for fear it will somehow invoke his presence. Harry, like us, found that avoiding his name simply gave him more power. And it is like that with David's death; avoiding the story and not speaking of the memories of David simply give the pain and heartache more power.

Hell, I take any chance I can get to speak of David! In fact I have noticed that some people, though they try to hide it, get uncomfortable when I mention his name. Those that knew him, who perhaps had not thought of the tragedy for quite some time, often react subtly like I have kicked them in the groin when his name flows from my lips without a moment's hesitation. Just this past week I spoke to one of his old coaches back in our hometown over the phone. We discussed many things, and of course David's name came up. When it did I could hear the all too familiar change in his voice. This guy is a big, strong, no nonsense kind of guy, but I could hear his voice crack and his words start to falter a bit. I acted as if I had not noticed and continued speaking freely about David and us and our lives. It actually did him some good I believe to hear how I had come to a place where I could speak of David without slipping into the depths of despair. But I have had the "advantage" of living with it constantly since he died. He had not. For him the pain of having lost David was still much fresher. He didn't live it every day so he had not grieved and come to stare that ugly accident down the way we have.

I love talking about David; I even don't mind relating the story of his accident to those that will listen. It helps me continue to move forward. If you have someone in your life who has lost someone, anyone, don't be afraid of invoking their memory. Though it may bring tears, those tears are healing. We want to speak of those that are gone. We have to; it's all we have left. Yes it hurts, it's supposed to. If it didn't it would mean we didn't care. But after a while the hurt becomes smiles and laughter about the wonderful person we all had the good fortune to have in our lives. Having a chance to speak to those that knew him is a gift to me. It keeps him alive. And it may help you too, to see that life has continued. So, do us all a favor. If he comes to mind, speak his name, please. He's always on my mind; it's nice to know he meant enough to you that you miss him too.

A TEAM MOVES FORWARD

    I think back to my days of childhood, running and playing with my friends, laughing at each other when we fell down or tripped, or got our wind knocked out of us, and I remember mostly us laughing and then getting on with playing. Occasionally someone would need to run home to mom and get a cut or scrape cleaned up, a Band-Aid applied, and then back they came. In a worst case scenario, someone got driven off to the doctors and then came back with a cool oversized white plaster cast that over the next six weeks would become a cool kind of canvas for everybody in school to draw and write on until it got cut away, and the injured party would be back to normal.

    I never entertained the idea that one of my playmates might fall down, get up seemingly fine, and then a few minutes later collapse in front of us all, and die. I'm not even sure I could have truly wrapped my head around the idea of one of my friends dying. But for the members of David's football team, all boys between 10 and 12 years of age, that was what they watched happen that fateful night. Suddenly the myth of invincibility all people under the age of 25 live under was torn asunder, and right there in front of them, the harsh realities of the tenuous nature of everyone's existence came home to them in a brutal and real way.

As I have written earlier, Leslie and I were very aware that we were not the only ones to lose David. This was especially true with his teammates. I had grown to know these boys very well in the time we spent together. I was the team's manager and as such I helped make sure they had the equipment they needed, Gatorade and oranges for the games, ran game time raffles to fund and arrange pizza parties after games, and roamed the sidelines during games offering encouragement to them all as they played and made sure all the things the coaches could not worry about during a game got taken care of. I believe the boys respected me, and I know I respected them. Thankfully, after David's death, the Team Mom stepped up and took over everything seamlessly, and the entire team rallied around us. But what about those young men, those boys, the children, what about them?

I have to say that at every turn the parents of David's teammates made great decisions for their kids. It started with the vigil they held at the field. The boys were encouraged to express themselves about how much they liked David and what he meant to them. They did craft projects to express their love for him and our family. At the funeral they all dressed in their team shirts, sat together as a team, and stood proud as the team they had become and that they knew David had loved so much. In the first couple of weeks they gave these young warriors every chance to deal with their confusion and loss in creative ways. And with our support and agreement, they got back to the football field to do what they loved; playing football.

The coaches never shied away from what had happened. They told the boys that what had happened to David was a freak accident, which it was, and that they needed to get back to doing what David would want them to do; play football. They gave them as much reassurance as they could, basically telling them to "get back on the horse." I imagine there are many who would disagree with this course of action, but I believed, as did the coaches, that they needed to see that life moves forward and that the best way to honor David, the player that never gave up, was to do what he surely would have done. Just 8 days after David died they were going to take the field again, against a team that would be there to win, and the best way they could pay tribute to David was to play their hardest. And at their coaches' urging, this is what they did. In fact, I believe in hindsight, the players were more successful at doing this than the coaches were.

    I still occasionally talk with David's head coach, a man I respect. This was not the coach that spoke at his funeral, but just like that man; he too lost the fervor to coach. After decades of being a coach, David's accident had changed the way he sees the game. We have discussed this, and I have tried to reassure him that we did not hold him responsible in any way for David's death. He hung in there for the rest of the season and I know coached again the next season in order to help the team move forward, both in the sport, and in life. But he no longer coaches.

    Of course the first game back was going to be very hard for the boys, and I knew this. I had a lot of love for these boys, I wanted to make sure these boys came through this experience with as little lingering heartache as possible. Because of this I showed up at their first game back. I didn't want to be a distraction, so I did not appear before the game. I let the coaches prepare the boys to move forward and play on their own. I decided that showing up at the start of the second half would be the right time. I strode over to the field just as play began in the third quarter. As I got close the players began to notice I was there. Those not on the field came rushing to the fence to hug me. Tears flowed on both sides of that fence, but my message stayed the same, go beat these guys for David. The electricity on the sideline became palpable. I was here for them, and they knew it. They felt like David was there with them. Coach asked me if I wanted to join them on the sidelines but I told him no, my place was in the stands with the other parents. He nodded his understanding. The players all wanted to show me how much it meant to them for me to be there by being all they could be on the field. And they delivered. The parents who all came by to pay their respects all made it clear that the team had come alive when I showed up. And in fact the boys went from losing that game to winning it very convincingly. It was amazing to watch these young men respond with their hearts and souls. Seeing the passion they had shared with David come alive on the field and lead them to victory was impressive. Midway through the fourth quarter they had the game in hand. I sat in the stands by myself, my baseball hat and sunglasses in place, and cried silently. These people who I sat amongst had made me proud to be associated with them. The coaches had given the team a great lesson in life; that you keep moving forward. The parents had allowed their sons to grieve openly and share their feelings and had supported them in the best possible ways. And the players? Well, they showed me their love for David by being the very best they could be and by not giving up.

 I came back to several games that year, and when I did there was always a marked improvement on the field. They didn't win every game, but they had a good season. There were a few of the boys whose heart to play never came back, and they stopped after that year. That of course is completely understandable. But they didn't give up immediately. They played on for a while and did not let tragedy get the best of them. Several of the other players are still playing and excelling on the teams they now play for. I know of several that to this day carry his #18 with them into every game. But whether they stopped playing or not the important thing was that they moved forward together. We all did. They helped me keep going as much as having me come to their games helped them. I think of them all often. I cherish the times we shared. And I am happy they all knew my boy and that he knew them.

 Go Vikings.

IN MY DREAMS

> *"I close my eyes, then I drift away, into the magic night I softly say.*
> *a silent prayer, like dreamers do, then I fall asleep*
> *to dream my dreams of you."*
> ~Roy Orbison

When I was in 2nd grade my Grandmother on my mom's side of the family died. I was about the same age as Abby was when David died. I remember hearing hushed conversations around the house for a couple of days before she passed away. She was a large woman in failing health, and she had fallen in her house and had been hospitalized. I knew things were serious, but I don't think I had any concept of what was actually happening. In hindsight it is obvious to me that my mother and father, and older siblings knew Nana might not survive the fall. To my parents credit, when she died they told me very quickly, and explained that she had not been in good health and her body just could not take the trauma.

My grandparents had been an important part of my life. They lived nearby and holidays and birthdays and lots of other times were spent at their homes and with them in attendance at ours. I remember being at the funeral parlor for the viewing, and seeing her, the first time I had seen a dead person, laid out in her casket looking very much alive, except she wasn't. I say that, because to me it is always off-putting to look at someone who has died. It's always somehow so obvious they are no longer alive. There is something about the incredible stillness of the body. Even when someone is asleep or unconscious there is still movement, imperceptible to the eye, but it's there, and somehow you know they are still alive. Nana was not. My sister had kept me entertained most of the time in an adjoining room so I wouldn't be a pest to the mourners. I remember the funeral vaguely. It was a rainy day. We all rode in a big black car to the cemetery. But other than those few details, I don't have many vivid memories of what went on. I sometimes ponder the fact that Abby was at the same emotional age when she lost David. I'm sure the memories of David's death are much more vivid to her because the two of them were so very close, but still, she perceived all that happened through a similar emotional awareness. I'm not sure why, but that saddens me and also comforts me at the same time.

What I do remember of my grandmother's death very vividly though, is the dream. I remember that there were lots of tears when Nana died, and I was starting to wonder if there was something wrong with me because I had not cried over her passing. No one had said anything to me about it. I had been reassured that it was okay to cry if I wanted to, but it was more of a fascination, this whole death thing, than it was a sadness to me at 7. But one night, about a week after the funeral, Nana came to me in a dream. Whether this was simply a 7 year-olds mind dealing with the loss any way it could, I can't say. I will say that I normally don't remember my dreams, and this particular one was amazingly vivid. Nana had come to me and held me. She walked to me easily in the dream, which was something she could not do in real life. She explained to me that she was very happy. She told me she loved me very much and that we would see each other again someday. She told me to be a good boy, and not to worry about not crying; she understood that I loved her. Then she kissed me and said goodbye. As she walked away, the tears came. I woke up crying. My mother quickly came to my bedside. She held me, and we cried together. My mother assured me that it was only a dream but that everything Nana had said was true. She kissed me and tucked me back into my bed. Somewhere deep inside I have always felt that if there was a moment in my life that I felt I had experienced anything close to a mystic experience, that dream was it.

Of course, after David died I could not stop thinking about the dream with my grandmother. There was a part of me that knew that if there was any justice in the world I would get a visit from my boy, telling me he was okay, he was happy, and that we would see each other again someday. That dream did not come. I have all sorts of rationale as to why it didn't, including the fact that I sat in his room one day and told him if he had to come visit somebody, to come to his mother and visit her, she needed it more than I did. When Leslie had a few dreams about David, I hung onto that as the reason he had not come to me, but I still was wounded by the fact I had not gotten a chance to see him again. Of course then I was looking for the dream, which probably kept it on the back burner of my mind.

Eventually I did dream of David, but not for at least 6 months after his accident. Which meant I went through Halloween, Thanksgiving, Christmas and my own birthday without having a dream about him. It was not until I had resignedly given up on ever having a dream about him, that he appeared. Coincidence? I think not. When he did show up the first time, it was a strange dream where we were on two different trains in some amusement park. He was having a fun time on his train, and I was having fun on mine, but we could not speak to each other. The trains kept getting closer to each other as the tracks would almost meet up, and then they would diverge again, and he seemed to be enjoying the fact we could not talk. It was a truly torturous dream, yet at the same time I heard him laugh and it did my heart good. Since then we have had many adventures together in the nether world. We have laughed and hugged and there are many mornings that I awaken to realize he's not really here, and though that waking moment of realization is always disheartening, the time we spend together is wonderful. Interestingly when we moved from California to Michigan, after about a week or so the David dreams increased exponentially for a while. I assume this was because after we left California there were not as many people around that made me think of him. The constant reminders I could find on every street corner of him in our old town were not there, so he was showing up in my dreams to sort of say, "Hey, I'm still here." It was good to know. The truth is he's always with me. But every once in a while it is nice to be in a place where the rules of the real world don't apply, and I get to giggle and play with my boy again.

    Dreams are good.

FALLING

In the immediate aftermath of a tragedy there are all sorts of emotional pitfalls a person has to beware of. There is the denial, anger, total desperation, the incredible desire to flee the situation and the complete loss of ability to connect with people. All of these have a multitude of complications that, if not addressed, can lead to real world consequences not just in the immediate, but for months, years, even decades down the road. Unfortunately they are not the only dangers lurking in the shadows waiting to surface and wreak havoc with your life. There is no doubt that many grievers suffer from a form of Post Traumatic Stress Syndrome not unlike what soldiers and survivors of major disasters deal with. Dreams that haunt us, insomnia, loss of appetite, nervousness and the inability to concentrate are all symptoms of the freshly bereaved. To some degree I suffered from all of these after David's sudden death. Time seemed to slip away and my memory became as porous as a chain link fence. People would tell me something and moments later it would be forgotten. My mind was so consumed with trying to deal with the incredible grief from moment to moment that it had no ability to grasp information and hang onto it. I started writing things down, when I could even remember to do that, so that I could get things done. It was like I had been hit with a short-term memory disease that allowed me no ability to retain information. As time moved forward this seemed to get better, but my ability to focus on what I was doing came and went with no warning. Looking back I realize there are huge pieces of my life during that time that I have no good memory of. I saw people who told me of things happening in their life that today I have no memory of. The description "going through life in a fog," is incredibly accurate.

Perhaps the most visible signs of this affliction were the bruises and stubbed toes that I seemed to constantly be suffering from. It seemed my coordination had left me over night. That I continued to drive without having a major accident is a minor miracle. And then one afternoon I suffered the proverbial "accident at home" that we always hear is way more likely to happen than a car accident.

It was early afternoon, and I was walking from the kitchen into my office at the house. I was not carrying anything, or eating, or being distracted by anything. I entered my office and side stepped a small box on the floor in front of my glass bookcase. Or so I thought. My right toe caught the corner of the box, and suddenly I was in a free fall. I reacted as quickly as I could, and at least was able to deflect myself enough to keep from smashing through the glass doors of my bookcase. But to do that it meant I had to go down straight to the floor onto my left knee. Now as I have already discussed I was quite heavy at the time, the full weight of my entire body falling was stopped on the wood floor with my knee, and my knee only. It was not a coordinated rolling fall or glancing blow, it was a solid impact. I fell to my side as the excruciating pain shot up my leg and set my knee on fire.

Now, having done my fair share of dancing and physical work over the years on stage I had suffered several sprains and contusions, and in my experience if I could get to my feet and keep the joint moving it would lessen the severity of the resulting injury. I immediately got to my feet and started moving around. I was in total shock. I'm not sure I had ever landed this hard in my life. But hey, I was on my feet and moving. I stumbled to the kitchen and kept flexing my knee. It burned, so I quickly made my way to the freezer and removed an ice pack I used for my shoulder from time to time. I wrapped it tightly around my knee and continued to move around. The pain began to lessen, and though I knew I had really banged it badly, it appeared that it was not broken and could support my substantial weight without any great additional pain. I was going to survive. I was going to be incredibly sore and might limp around for a few days, but it was going to be okay.

Over the course of the next hour it continued to improve. I had to run out to do some errands and stop at the bank for cash, but the pain had subsided enough under the constant application of ice packs that I concluded I was well enough to get in the car and do what I had to. It was then I made a choice that in hindsight I realize was not a good one. I had a couple of different neoprene knee supports I have used from time to time, and I figured sliding one on might be good support for the knee. I removed the ice pack, slid on the knee brace and stood up. Not too bad, I could walk okay, the knee flexed pretty well. I could do this. I called Leslie at work and sheepishly admitted I had fallen in the office, but assured her I was okay, and that I was going out.

For the next 45 minutes I drove around town and did everything I needed to from the convenience of my front seat. It was my left knee that I had injured, so I just put it in one position and left it there while I drove. As I got out of the car when I got home, I noticed it had gotten pretty stiff and it felt a little warm, so I came inside and peeled off the neoprene knee brace.

My knee started to swell and it started to hurt. Apparently, the brace was a bad idea, and now without any compression, it was swelling up badly. I called Leslie and told her it was starting to hurt and I might go to urgent care. I called her back 5 minutes later and told her I was going to go to the emergency room. 5 minutes more and I called her to tell her she needed to come home because I wasn't going be able to drive myself. About the time she got to her car in the parking lot at work, I was on her phone again telling her an ambulance was on it's way to me because I could no longer move at all and I did not think she could help me get to the car. When EMS arrived my toes were contorting from the pain. They loaded my fat ass up onto a gurney and rolled me out to the truck.

    Let me just say this was the first in a series of things that afternoon that were torturous in a non-physical way. It had only been about a month since I had seen a team of EMS guys load my son up on a gurney. I now was lying on my back in a truck just like the one that had taken David to the ER. When we arrived at the ER, they unloaded me and rolled me through the same doors he was taken through into the same ER. Here I was, in pain, lying in the same ER, seeing a few of the same nurses that had been there the night my boy died. It was downright surreal. The pain was excruciating, but apparently because of all the other things bouncing around in my head, I neglected to ask for painkillers. Finally after about 15 minutes of lying there writhing in pain, Leslie asked if they had given me anything for the pain. I shook my head "no." We called over the nurse, and when they realized they had neglected to give me anything, they quickly gave me a big old dose of morphine.

    Well that did the trick, my pain started to fade and I started to swim in a drug-induced joyride. Leslie had to get Abby from school, so I assured her I was fine, and off she went. No sooner had she left the ER then a wave of nausea started to sweep through my insides. I called over the nurse and told her I might be sick. She assured me that morphine could do that sometimes and handed me one of those cute little half-moon shaped things they give people to throw up into. I looked at the tiny little silver tray and thought, "Wow, these people have never seen me hurl." But, before I could tell the nurse I needed something bigger, up came lunch. I'd like to say I got it all in the barf tray, but before anything had left my mouth I went unconscious. Apparently the morphine had made my blood pressure crash, and I passed out mid puke. I awoke covered in my lunch, and the tray lying at my side. It was like sophomore year of college all over again.

The nurse didn't seem to bat an eye as she cleaned me up. We called Leslie and told her to stop home and get me some fresh clothes. It was turning into a really special day. Then suddenly it was time for x-rays, and in a few moments I found myself being rolled into the radiology room. I asked the technician if they had more than one x-ray room, and he said no, this was it. I told him it was weird being in the same room my son had been in a month earlier. He knew the whole story, he had heard about it from the other x-ray technician and said they knew my son was in trouble as soon as they saw the x-rays. As Rod Serling would say, I had now entered the Twilight Zone. I don't remember a whole lot more after that, partially because of the morphine, and partially because I think I tuned everything out because it was all just too much to process.

The next thing I really remember was being told that somehow I had not broken it, and the pain was due to severe swelling of the bursa under the knee. They said they could drain some fluid, but felt it would be better to just drug me up and if the swelling didn't go down in the next 24 hours to come back and they would drain it. I got a leg brace, crutches and was sent home.

I healed up over the next week or two, and my knee got better, but thanks to being immobile, I got to sit on my butt a lot and think about David.

Interestingly, Leslie also fell, about three weeks after I did. Same kind of careless accident as I had. She turned around in the dining room and tripped over her own feet. She didn't hurt her knees, but she tore an old surgery scar in her stomach and had to have a small hernia operation to repair it. She of course knew my joy at being in the same x-ray room David had lain in, and she had no interest in laying in the same operating room we had gone in to visit David on the night of his accident. She scheduled her operation at a local surgical center to avoid that scenario.

In hindsight it's obvious we were both suffering from lack of concentration and our ability to function normally, though we believed ourselves fine, was seriously diminished in the months after David's death. All those people that tell you to take care of yourself are not just being nice. They know that it's a perilous time after a sudden trauma like losing your child. "Taking care of yourself" means more than getting sleep and eating right. It means watching every step you take, and every move you make. It means being aware that you are not 100% after something like that, and accidents happen much more frequently. If you are in that place of grief where you are consumed by your thoughts of loss, take extra care not to fall. You've got enough on your plate to deal with without being physically injured as well.

WHAT SHE LOST

"It is hard to be brave, when you're only a very small animal."
~Winnie the Pooh

  Losing David at the age of ten was something so horrific and crushing words cannot describe it. There is an unnatural aura about seeing something you brought into this world leave before you do. There is nothing that compares to the loss of hopes and dreams, not for yourself, but for your child, that dwarfs anything else I have ever gone through. That being said, as much as Leslie and I lost when David died, his little sister Abby lost something just as devastating from her perspective. Her big brother was her protector, best friend, coconspirator and so many other things it is impossible to understand them all. Considering she was only 7 when he died, I have no doubt that she didn't understand the depth of what had happened either.
  Abby was born when David was just a little over 2 years of age. We had prepared him for her coming arrival by including him in everything. He was saying her name for months before she was born in a cute little rhythm that emphasized the wrong syllable "ab-BY" which he knew used to make us laugh. Before the two of them ever laid eyes on each other he was smitten with her. After she came into this world there was nothing he would not do for his little sister.

From David's point of view he was the big brother, and no one was going to take advantage of his little sister. He would show her how things worked, help her learn to read and count. He taught her about the pets, showed her video games. He loved her without limits. I would venture to say the feeling was mutual. Everything she saw in her world came through David, even the ways she attempted to connect with Leslie and myself.

Abby saw early on that David enjoyed sports and competition. When she got to an age when she too could play a sport she gravitated towards softball. She had spent many afternoons watching me coach David's team when he first started playing baseball, so it was the obvious choice for her. She and David had both tried soccer when they were really young, but that had too much running for David, and since he had no interest in that neither did Abby. I coached her softball team the first year she played and she tried hard, and was pretty good at it, but the next year when I decided not to coach and only attend practices and games, her interest in the game waned quickly. She wasn't there for the sport; she was there because dad was coach. She had learned that from her brother.

David had this influence on her in everything. If David wanted to try fishing, so did she. If David wanted to try cooking, so did she. If David was going to be playing football, then she wanted to put on that cheerleader outfit and cheer him on like the others girls cheered on their brothers. She was the ideal little sister, following her brother's lead, doing the things he did because it looked fun and her best friend was doing it too. It extends even to this day. There are things she knows David enjoyed which she has tried simply because she knew he enjoyed it.

Now I don't mean to mislead you and make it sound like they never had disagreements. They did. Abby is a very spirited and strong willed little girl, and as is only right, as she got older she learned exactly where his buttons were, and she learned a billion different ways of pushing them. But she wasn't pushing his buttons to make him angry or to hurt him. No, Abby used her tools of annoyance to make sure he was paying attention to her. It was never to make her brother go away, but rather to engage him when he seemed to be playing his PlayStation too long without her. I was the youngest of four children in my family so I recognized this technique because I had used it so often when I was younger. It used to drive David crazy, and you could always tell it was being used, even if she was doing it stealthily, by the annoyed and elongated "ABBEEEEE!" David would holler when she finally got to him. But those few instances aside, they were best buds.

    The connection and symbiotic relationship went much deeper than simply the things she wanted to try. David was Abby's thermostat to Leslie and I as well. From the moment she came out of the womb, David was her emotional guide through everything. He was there to help her understand not only how things worked, but to gauge what was going on around her and let her know when to behave. It was almost like he was her self-appointed guide dog. When Leslie or I were getting angry with them for being kids, it was David who knew when the line was in danger of being crossed. He would give Abby the high sign to cool it before we would blow our stacks. Because of this Abby's intuition was tuned in to David and not us. This made for a very difficult time after he died. Not only was she horrified of bringing up something that would set Leslie or I off with tears over David, but she also didn't know the warning signs of when we were going to lose our patience with her. And in all honesty, I have to confess that in the months after David died we were not the most consistent of parental units. Our emotions and ability to cope with anything other than the loss we had suffered meant we were probably more akin to Sally Fields' "Sybil" than we were to the reliable parents she was used to. So there were many moments of tension and discord between the three of us.

These oft times epic like battles of wills and desires went on for quite some time. And to be honest, there are still reverberations to this day, four years later. But what didn't stop happening was our communication. We talked about it all non-stop. All too often when a sibling dies the parents will orphan their other children. Not only do those children then suffer the loss of their brother or sister, but they lose their parents to the grief as well. Luckily for our family, Leslie and I were both on the same page. If we erred when it came to dealing with the grief, we erred in Abby's favor. If it was a choice between what was best for us, or what was best for Abby, we would swallow our own needs long enough to make sure Abby was getting what we felt was the right thing for her. And to our little lady's credit, she returned this love and care without even knowing it.

Abby was always a good student, but after David's death she really worked extra hard. David had been an excellent student and had been designated a "Gifted and Talented" student with the tests they use to determine such things. The year after David died, Abby too took that same test, and beamed with pride when her scores came back higher than what her brother had scored. She was always a good reader and creative writer for her age, but it was her math scores that went up tremendously after David died. David had possessed a real gift for math, the kind of kid who could just "see it" and didn't understand how others didn't. Abby was always good at math, but after he died, she worked extra hard at it, is if to try and make up for the fact that our little math genius had died.

When it came to expressing her feelings over David's death, Abby was a bit more reserved, I'm sure in part because she was afraid it would get her parents crying, which is hard for a child to see. But she talked about him a lot, and we would often relate tales of what David used to do and laugh about his quirks. We didn't want to turn David into a saint in her eyes. We wanted to keep him very real, so the shadow of his life and death stayed in perspective and never threatened to be more important than the fact she was still living her life. She also spent two sessions at Comfort Zone Camp, a weekend outing where she got to play and learn about her emotions with other children that had lost parents or siblings. These two weekends were very helpful in showing her that she was not alone. It validated to her that what she was feeling was natural, and I think it also made her realize that what she had at home was two very loving parents who were struggling but loved her very much. It was a delicate balancing act, at times we were more successful than others in navigating the emotional currents, but now 4 years later, I'm confident in saying we all stayed in the boat and made it to shore.

But the journey is not complete. We learned early on that because Abby was so young when David died, and her emotional development still had a long way to go. Her dealing with David's death will continue and change as she gets older and her feelings will develop as she becomes more aware of what she feels. We've had several instances since where a question about what all happened bubbles to the surface. She doesn't seem hesitant to ask these days when one does come up, and Leslie and I try to answer her as honestly as we can.

We still talk about David all the time. We celebrated when Abby became older than David was when he died. Occasionally a memory of things David did will come to her out of the blue, and often it's something Leslie and I were unaware of. It always brings a smile to all our faces. Sometimes when she can't sleep, she tells us she's thinking about David. This usually gets what she wants, which is to stay up a little later and talk with us, maybe flip through a photo album or go through the memory box that she decorated at the hospital after David's accident. I had my suspicions that she had begun to use "I can't sleep, I'm thinking about David," as an excuse to not go to bed. It was just about a month or so ago that I called her on that one. I let her know when her mom was not around that I knew it had become something she knew she could say that would get us to pay attention to her. She couldn't help herself but smile and laugh when I "truthed" her. She assured me that sometimes it was real, but she also copped to the fact she used it sometimes to get what she wanted. The next time she tried it when her mom was around she looked at me, and we both busted out laughing. That moment more than anything we have gone through told me we were all doing okay.

The three of us share a much different relationship today than we ever would have if David had lived. It has changed us. Some of the aspects are probably for the worse, but much is for the better. She knows us much better than most kids know their parents. We've shared emotions and thoughts about life and death that most kids don't share with their parents between the ages of 7 and 11. But she lost her best friend and companion. And as an only child now, she is entitled to hear the things she would have heard from David from somebody. Certain things you have to hear from people who love you and who you trust. Of course we still have the teenage years on the near horizon, and who knows what that will bring, but going into it we feel good about our family, and our relationships with our daughter. After all, it was Abby that was our walking and breathing example that life goes forward after David died. I thank the universe every day that we have her. I don't know what David dying would have done to me if she weren't here.

Daddy loves you Abby. Always have. Always will.

PROTECTION IS A FANTASY

"Security is mostly a superstition. It does not exist in nature, nor do the children of men as a whole experience it. Avoiding danger is no safer in the long run than outright exposure. Life is either a daring adventure, or nothing."

~Helen Keller

There is a difference between taking precautions and protection. "Precautions" are real measures that an intelligent person uses to minimize the potential damage that can occur while undertaking any activity. We learn many of these precautions when we are young, looking both ways before crossing a street, never running with scissors, not using the word "fat" and "mother" in the same sentence. As parents we spend much of our time teaching our children these things with the idea that it will offer them "protection" from the world's dangers. And therein lies the conundrum. You see, "precautions" are tangible proactive procedures that one can quantify, demonstrate and utilize again and again. The disconnect is that regular use of these precautions leads to the belief that we, our children, those we love are now "protected." There's only one problem; "protection" is not an obtainable goal.

"Protection" is in fact not a reliable thing, not in the universe we live in. A person can be protected for a period of time, but it is not a permanent state of being. The fact is that at any given moment, no matter how well tested and thought out the precautions you take are, no matter how many years these same precautions have shielded others who have come before and may shield those that come after, on any given day they may not be enough. You can call it "accident," "randomness," or like Jeff Goldblum's character in JURASSIC PARK called it, "chaos," but it is what renders the word "protection" fantasy. Trust me, I learned this the hard way.

When David came home and told me he wanted to play football at the age of seven, I honestly had two reactions. The first was one of amusement and happiness. I have always loved the sport. As a child I loved playing touch football, flag football and even those reckless "unprotected" games of tackle as a young man. I remember one such game very fondly from college during a huge snowstorm where we could barely move through the 2 feet of snow on the ground and the heavy snow that was still falling. And I have always loved watching football games, whether in a stadium or on TV. Yes there was an unmistakable leap of joy in my soul when my boy came home and announced he wanted to play football. But concurrent with the thrill of that father son connection, there was a voice in my head that said, "Wait a second, football? With pads and helmets and all that? Are you kidding me, you're only 7?" Leslie and I talked about it quite a bit. I did some research online, and watched some videos of kids that age "playing" football. Interestingly enough the statistics pointed to football, especially at that age, with all the equipment they wear, and the speed at which they move, and the body weight they carry, was among the safest of youth sports to play. Unlike baseball and soccer, where there was very limited safety equipment, in football everything vital seemed protected. And after watching the videos of youth players colliding into each other rather clumsily at that age, we decided it was probably as safe as anything else. I also knew that David had inherited my eating gene, so getting him involved in a sport where conditioning and exercise were part of the program could only be a good thing. As the years passed and David got bigger, and things got more physical, even he said, "Maybe just one or two more years dad." Before the start of what would be his final season, at age 10, we decided that, to take further precautions and "protect" him, we would buy the newest and safest helmet that was available. It was an extra expense, a considerable one, but we were sure it would offer him greater "protection." It didn't work.

We all live under the fallacy that our families are safe, but protection is not authentic. It is no more real today than it was 100 years ago, or 10,000 years ago. Mine are not simply the bitter words of one of the "unlucky ones" who is trying to scare and deflect my anger at the rest of humanity; sadly it is the ugly truth. And it is one of the most devastating things to deal with when unforeseen tragedy strikes. That is because this false sense of security is a necessity in all our lives. Without it we would never let our children learn to ride a bicycle, or skateboard. We would never ourselves get behind the wheel of a car, or swim in the ocean with all those dangerous sharks, or step out of the shower dripping wet. If we did not live under this false sense of safety, the idea that all those bad things happen to other people but not to us, we could not go forth and live. I have been a great practitioner of this self-delusion my entire life. Perhaps it was that self-delusion that allowed me to let my son play football. Believe me, it's one of those big guilt things I will be living with for the rest of my life. But I have come to understand that if I was misguided in my belief that our family was safe, it's not something I can or should punish myself for. We all do it. And it is a good thing. It is essential for survival. In fact, one of the most important parts of moving forward through our grief was rebuilding that illusion so that we could live fully again and not merely survive.

It is this loss of a safety net, the evaporation of the mirage of protection, which often cripples people in grief. Often this loss of the feeling of security is compounded by other feelings of guilt. It is especially difficult for those who lose a loved one through suicide or irresponsible behavior by someone. Those people that are left behind, in trying to make rhyme or reason out of the tragedy, wallow in this loss of security, believing so strongly that their family should have been safe from disaster that they blame anyone they can, but especially themselves, for the crushing loss. They look at the world around them and see only that everyone else is safe, and that because of their "failure" the one they love is gone. But it's not true. Since David's death I am often stunned at how much pain and suffering is all around us. Most of us, certainly I, prefer not to dwell on it. Perhaps I felt that by seeing the hurt around me I would welcome it into my life. Of course that is crazy talk. The world is cruel and random. Some things are not in our control. Being able to see that is the first step forward to rebuilding.

In my mind, our family's canopy of false safety has been repaired. Why would I want to rebuild an illusion? Quite simply, if one wants to move forward that illusion is a necessity to keep oneself from being crippled by fear. And though it has been repaired, it's not perfect. There is a huge tear down the middle of it, which has been stitched back together, often hastily and imperfectly. Reality and fear occasionally drip through, but I had to rebuild it as best I could, Abby's future depends on it. It makes me sad to know that at such an early age her canopy of presumed safety already has such a rip in it, but she has many years ahead, and hopefully hers will one day show minimal signs of past damage. For me, I can live with the occasional drip of reality. That makes me appreciate the fact that we have been able to move forward all the more. It is that rip that makes me want to reach out to others who are suffering and try to show them that there is life here waiting to be lived. David used to get very frustrated and cry at himself when he caused discord in the family. After his death I often had the vision of him watching how sad we were and being angry with himself that his death had caused us such anguish. I had to find a way to move forward, for him and for us. I know he would want us to live fully. None of us get out of here alive, and I chose to live while I'm still here. So to live, I need that overhang of protection, even if it is just an illusion.

TWO CARS

When David was suddenly ripped from our family, I was lost. I know, not exactly a revelation there. I went into survival mode, and put up walls, got angry, stood in the living room and screamed at the universe, held onto those I love, and looked for some sign as to where to go now so that I could somehow keep going.

There was no road map. It quickly became apparent that this had affected Leslie, Abby and I in different ways, and the journey through this nightmare would be different for each of us. No two people react to such a massive loss the same way. There were long stretches where Leslie and I were simply surviving in the same house. I knew she loved me. She knew I loved her. But in this ordeal there was not going to be any "leaning on each other" because both of us were using everything we had to keep it together.

We focused on doing what we could for Abby, and talked and cried a lot. The smartest thing we did was to not hide our tears. We shared great love. There was, thankfully, no blame to be assigned, and though I'm sure there were times she didn't want to see my tears, we knew that the other needed room to find their own way through the grief. We got into the habit of checking in with each other. "How you doing?" The answers weren't long or detailed, they were quick and to the point; "I'm doing okay," "I cried a lot today," "I'm here."

Our son had died in October, just as we were heading into the holiday season. The idea of all the upcoming holiday parties and activities was horrifying. But we also had a bunch of friends who had rallied around us, and who were there for us when we needed them most. There were some events we simply had to do, often for our daughter. So, much like co-existing in the same house, we took the same approach to parties and such. We would arrive together, but in separate cars. That way when either one of us could not bear to stay any longer, we were free to go on our own terms.

I'll admit, the first time Leslie suddenly needed to get out, she just bolted, and it was hard for me. Seeing her just turn and walk out the door without saying goodbye initially felt wrong. After all, we had always been a team, making our decisions together.

What were the other people thinking?

Did they think our relationship was in trouble like so many others who had lost a child?

I certainly understand how people get lost, and lose each other when a child dies. But to be quite frank, I didn't care if our friends understood or not. This was not their marriage, and they had not lost their child.

In the middle of it all someone told me it was okay to be selfish. If there was ever going to be a time in your life where the people who loved you would understand you being a bit less than cordial, or even a downright asshole, it was now. You do what you have to do for yourself. The real friends would get it, and those that didn't? Good riddance.

I came to realize that when I got home, Leslie was still there. She left because the feeling of being overwhelmed would come on mid sentence, and for survival's sake, she just had to get out. And it is a testament to our friends that they understood. They gave us the space to do what we needed to do in order to survive. I will love them forever for that.

This arrangement went on for almost a year. Slowly but surely, we started to get back in sync. If there was any doubt, we'd take two cars, but when we realized we were starting to leave at the same time, we dropped back to just one car.

Now, more than four years down the road, we again navigate the social world in tandem. It's not the same as it was before, but we have rebuilt our avenues of communication. In many ways, we know each other better today than we did before. I think we probably respect each other's individuality more. There is a bond between us that could only be forged through hardship. I imagine it's not unlike the respect and trust built between comrades in arms that go through battle together.

We have seen the worst of it, and survived.

We were lucky to have built a great trust between us before our son died, because every bit of that trust was put to the test.

I remember us having a conversation long before his death that if there were ever a tragedy, like a child dying, we hoped it would bring us closer together instead of driving us apart. We had had no concept of how naive that point of view was, until after. But as time moves forward, and the hunger to live life returns and blooms inside us, individually and as a couple, I understand that we have been blessed, and are indeed very fortunate.

I understand how easily we could have lost each other. I can't point to one thing that got us through to a place where we could move forward. Maybe it's the love we share for our daughter. Perhaps it's because we had parents whose relationships ingrained in us that it's never easy, and sometimes damn near impossible. Maybe it's because for us, the love we share is worth it. Maybe it's because she's the only one who really understands what I've been through.

Or maybe, it was the two cars.

BIRTHDAYS

It's no secret that the day of the year that holds the most dread for parents who have lost a child is the birthday. That annual marker, which in most cases is a day to celebrate another year in the march forward to being a grown human being. But for those of us who have lost a child, it is a day that represents all that could have been. It makes no difference how old your child was when they died; there is always, from a parent's perspective, things that were yet to be.

Since my boy died at the tender age of 10, the list is massive. He was still at the stage where he was pretty much ignorant of girls and the joys and heartbreak they would bring to his life. Or maybe it would have been boys. I don't know, and neither did he yet. The whole sexual awakening thing hadn't had a chance to happen. So his "first love" never happened. Which means no first kiss.

He never knew what it was to be a teenager. Though, like any kid we had disagreements over too much fast food or what he watched on TV, for the most part my son still saw Leslie and I the way young kids always see their parents; icons of all they hoped to be. He never had the chance to come to the realization that we were just people with problems and faults all our own. He never had that pull to do something he knew we would really not agree with. His world revolved around making us happy, and doing what we thought he should. The rebellion against our parents that we all go through, that which makes us who we are going to be, never had a chance to happen.

Ironically, because of his death, his younger sister Abby has seen that mom and dad are not perfect. She has seen us cry, and be petty and even mean at times because of the grief we encountered. She has had conversations with us that go far beyond what she would have had with us because life was cruel to her, and took away her co-conspirator in this family dynamic. We have shared feelings and thoughts with her, so that she knows the crazy thoughts that might be bouncing around in her head are normal. She still has lots to learn as she grows, and the questions she encounters and develops in relationship to his death will be plentiful. Thankfully, Leslie and I are aware of this, which is why our communication with her is beyond what it would have been had he still been here.

My boy will never know what it means to learn to drive and experience the freedom that a first driver's license gives you. He will never go off to college, and be on his own. He will never have the realization Mare Winningham's character has in ST. ELMO'S FIRE about just how good a peanut butter and jelly sandwich can taste when you realize it came from your own refrigerator, in your own apartment. He will never know true love, or marriage, or success at his chosen career, or even what that career might have been. He will never know the incredible joy of holding your own child in your arms, feeling their warm breath upon your cheek, the gentle beat of their heartbeat, and the joyous music of their unbridled laugh.

Of course these are things I will never get to see him do either. I am acutely aware that wrapped in and around my sadness for him never getting to experience these things, is the selfish loss I feel at never seeing him experience these things. I lost my only son. And though we had a chance to share many father/son moments like learning to throw a baseball, ride a bike, play poker and build an X-Wing fighter out of Lego, there are far more things we had yet to share together that will never happen. Teaching him to cut the lawn, and drive, and sharing a beer are all things we will never experience together.

I will never see him push away from us and become his own man, and will never experience the satisfaction of having him come back to us asking advice for something like helping to get his new baby to sleep.

I will never know the comfort of knowing as I grow old that he is there to help us maneuver old age and rely on him to make sure the old man isn't "losing the farm" to some conman preying on my addled senses.

Of course there are things I know of the life he did lead that bring some solace to these lost shared moments. I know that when he died my son had never truly known loneliness, or hunger or heartache. He had never had his heart broken beyond repair by the cruel actions of the world around him. His life was one of joy and happiness, filled with wonder and the unconditional love of a younger sister who he took great pride in protecting and guiding through the world he had become so learned at moving through. And he had two parents that believed he could do anything, and encouraged him in all things he wanted to try, even the one thing that beyond understanding took him from us, football.

Yes, it's the birthdays that bring all those things back to your mind. The things that "could have been" are among the hardest of things to forget and move forward from when you lose your child, no matter at what age it happens. It makes one ponder who he might be today. How the years since his death would have shaped and changed him, and what he would have become are the questions that will haunt me every day, but especially on his birthdays. Maybe I should try to just celebrate that on this date, 14 years ago, a young man came into this world that would change who I was, what I would become. His life continues to shape me, and will for as long as I draw breath in this wonderful and horrible thing we call life.

I miss you pal.
Happy Birthday.

GETTING OUT OF DOGDE

> *"All changes are more or less tinged with melancholy, for what we are leaving behind is part of ourselves"*
> -Amelia Barr

There came a time after David died when it became obvious that, in order for us to truly move forward with our lives, we needed to leave the town that had been so comforting to us after his death. It meant leaving our friends that had become family to us over the last twenty plus years, even if that meant leaving behind people who needed us as much as we needed them. It meant leaving behind what had been my life's work and pursuit. It meant taking a leap of faith that the real road forward to joy laid not in the glorious past we had built, but onward to a strange new land, full of new possibilities and opportunities and uncertainty.

We had come to this town when David was only three. We had left the congested San Fernando Valley of Los Angeles because David and Abby would be starting school soon and the schools in LA did not offer the things we valued for our children's education. We had toyed back then with the idea of staying where we were and going the private school route, but realized any money we spent on private education could be put into getting a larger home, in a safer neighborhood, where the public schools were as good as the private ones we could afford to send them to. Just over the line of LA county was a place that fit all the criteria; Simi Valley. It was no more than twenty five minutes from the crowded floor of the Valley, but the schools were good, and the community had the feel of the kind of places Leslie and I had grown up. Of course this was still Southern California, and that meant small lots, with many people per square mile, but the homes were well cared for, and the people had a belief that family was paramount. This was where we decided to settle.

As David and Abby grew they made great friends. Leslie and I made friends with the neighbors, the couple behind us becoming as good friends as we've had as a couple. We supported the schools, the sports the kids played in and I found a great little theater where I could get on stage and sing and dance in their musicals. We went camping together with friends, and became part of something bigger than us, a community of people dedicated to raising kids well. It was home. We were very happy. Life was very good.

Seven years in, there was that one horrible night at the football field, and David died. Everything we had invested in this town of people and friends came running towards us, arms stretched wide, wanting to do anything they could to help usher us through this nightmare. People genuinely wanted to help. I'm sure some did it not only out of the want to do the right thing for one of their own, but also because somewhere deep inside they were so thankful that it had not happened to their family, they felt an obligation to thank the universe by helping us. I say this not out of meanness, but because even after all we've been through, when I hear of something horrible happening to others, I give a little thanks to the cosmos it was not us this time, and look to see how I can help. But whatever their motivation, the outpouring of support was staggering.

There was the rally at the football field where David had perished that was attended by a couple of thousand people. There was the fund started for our family to help us out financially. The local high schools played a charity touch-football game between the cheerleaders and donated the money raised to David's fund, and none of them even knew us personally. Thankfully, we were lucky enough to have good health insurance and life insurance, so we were not in need of the funds, but we were able to turn around in the next couple of years and funnel that money back to worthy causes in the community and around the world in David's name. It made us feel good to be able to help others in David's name. The football league arranged to have meals delivered to us. In fact they had arranged to have meals delivered for 18 weeks. We had to tell them to stop after a few weeks, because even though it was incredibly sweet and helpful, getting back to making meals and doing for ourselves was part of what we needed to do to try and find our way back to the road forward. The theater where I had been performing held a dinner to show their love and support to us. His school planted a tree in his name. The football team retired his Jersey and number #18, never to be worn again. The Baseball field where he played had a banner with him on it urging people to "Live, Love, Laugh." The love and support was staggering.

All of this and so much more over the next few years made me love Simi Valley as much as any place I had ever been in my life. This was after all, the place David had grown up. Every street corner, every store, everything about this place said David. Unfortunately, though that was very comforting and familiar and wonderful in the time right after his death, as time stretched forward into the future, it became part of the problem as well.

We were moving forward, grieving and doing all the things we had to do so that our family unit could get back to the cohesive unit that it had been when there were four of us, with just the three of us. But every morning when I drove Abby to school, we went by the football field he died on. Every time I went shopping, I saw the workers in the store that knew him and loved him. The dry cleaner, who had donated to his football team, seemed to be holding back tears every time I took one of Leslie's suits in for cleaning. The tree the school had planted was growing bigger, and it reminded me every morning when I dropped off Abby that David was not here anymore. There were people I would see all the time around school or other places that no longer knew what to say to us. Though we were living with not having David every day, others only thought of it when they saw us, and you could see the pain, that to them, was still very fresh. I was starting to long for a place where everything I saw and did was not defined by an event that could reduce me to tears if I gave it enough time to get a foothold on my emotions. I started to think that maybe a fresh road forward in a place where we were not defined by this horrible tragedy wouldn't be so bad.

Anyone who has gone through a sudden tragedy like ours will tell you that the urge to run away is very strong. And it's not a rational thing. In the year after David died the urge to up and run, and never stop, was always right there. Of course I knew that I couldn't run away from the pain, and that running away from Leslie and Abby would only mean more pain to me and to them. But this feeling, the urge to make an educated move to give a new perspective on this different chapter in our family, was not the same thing. This was more taking back the power from the tragedy. This was a way to take control over something in our lives after so much of that control had been ripped from us in one tragic moment. And I had a strong desire to send the message to Abby that her life was not going to be defined by the loss of her brother. She was not going to go through the rest of her days in school as the girl whose older brother had died. The road ahead was hers to live on her terms. She deserved that. We all do.

And there was even more to it than that.

Six months after David died, our best friends and neighbors in town, the people who took Abby the night of the accident, received their own devastating news. The dad,

Matt, who was a few years younger than me, had received what I can only refer to as neglectful care, and by the time the proper care was taken, it resulted in a diagnosis of cancer that was at an advanced stage. All the time we were healing, and finding a way forward, we had to watch our best friends deal with a disease that a little over two years later would take Matt from them. It seemed to me like sadness and heartache had not only visited our wonderful little town, but it had pitched its tent right in our neighborhood, between our houses. During those two years we lived a lot. We shared hopes, tears, and more than a few times Matt and I held up the proverbial "bird" to death and gave it a hardy "Fuck You." Matt helped us survive David's death. I'd like to think we helped see them through the tragedy that was unfolding for their family. I would not trade those few years for anything. But it also made the drive to set a new course even stronger.

A few months before Matt would lose his battle to cancer, an opportunity presented itself to Leslie. She came home and mentioned the chance to relocate to Michigan. She had no idea how I would respond. My industry, show business, was the reason I had come to California twenty years earlier, and she did not know if I would have any desire to leave the pursuit of fame and fortune behind. If I remember correctly the conversation was quick, and I almost immediately said, "Let's do it." I believe I agreed to the change of scene so quickly Leslie didn't trust I was serious. But we set the move in motion, and as we planned our escape to calmer seas, we shared in Matt's last few months.

I'm glad we got to say goodbye to him. I'm glad we were there to hold onto them all as they tried to deal with such a horrible loss. There were lots of tears, and jokes about how Matt and David were looking down on us laughing at how we were all crying like babies. After Matt passed I was really ready to go. So, we went about selling our house and going on our new adventure. A few short months later, after one last 4th of July together in our neighbors' back yard and pool, and one last round of setting off fireworks illegally in the street in Matt and David's honor, we got on a plane and left.

The relocation was challenging for all of us, but I'm happy to report that it was the right move. We share David's story with those who seem interested, but it's different now. It's something that happened to us back there, where we used to live. It is on our terms when we want to share it. We all had to adjust to new ways of doing things and new environments. (Michigan and Southern California have slightly different climates and seasons, you know!) But the move has been a good thing, and we all seem to be thriving in this new chapter of our lives. New opportunities have developed, and life is happening again. And in the basement here in Michigan, David's retired football jersey hangs surrounded by pictures of our time in Simi Valley. David's urn sits atop our piano. We speak of him often, and I know that if he is anywhere, he is here with us, urging us forward in our lives. We didn't run away from our nightmare, we stood our ground, gathered the strength those around us provided, got our bearings, and then decided for the sake of us all, to make a change, and get the Hell out of Dodge.

LETTING GO OF EXPECTATIONS

"If the condition of grief is nearly universal, its transactions are exquisitely personal."
~Meghan O'Rourke

Grief is universal. Grief is individual. Both of those statements are 100% true. They seem to be at odds with each other, but they are not. The reason for this is because they speak to two totally different things. The first statement is about the fact we all experience grief when someone important dies, the second speaks to the process of grief that we must travel through in order to move forward. That process is different for everyone. You may lose a 10-year-old son named David as I did, playing football, with a little sister named Abby, a wife named Leslie, for a teamed named "the Vikings," and yet what you experience on your grief journey will be different than mine. There are certain stages of grief that most people will experience, but the time at which they affect you, or even if they ever do affect you, will be different. Some stages will last longer for you; some will be harder for me to deal with. Some of your reactions, or mine, may be unusual because of our lives leading up to that moment and our experiences with grief in our past. The point is, everyone who tells you exactly what you are going to feel or experience is going to be wrong, INCLUDING YOURSELF! There are no absolutes, except that it will be difficult, and that you must go through it to emerge on the other side, capable of moving forward.

I thought I knew myself pretty well when tragedy struck. And though looking back now I can see that what I have been through is very true to who I am, there were steps along the way that I didn't really expect, or that I would have told you, "That won't happen to me." I would have been wrong. And compounding the problems I faced, and still face, by giving myself expectations of how I "should" be reacting only makes the stress worse. So I tell you now, be good to yourself, and get rid of your expectations of how you should act. You will have people laying horrible expectations on you. "It's been two months, get over it!" "You've got to forget about it and move on." "I just went out and bought another dog, problem solved." They will be hurtful, ignorant and, though they don't realize it, mean and uncaring. I repeat: no one can tell you what you will feel, INCLUDING YOURSELF!

We live our lives preparing for what is to come, and we practice our actions and reactions so that we can traverse our daily lives as smoothly as possible. But you can't practice for grief. And the other thing that will be a real bitch is that even if you have grieved for someone in the past, each new experience with grief will be different from the last one. Yes that's right, even if you have successfully maneuvered through the dark forest of grief and emerged on the other side before, every journey is different, and the map you wrote as you made the trip last time will not necessarily make the next journey any easier. In fact, the last journey through grief may rear its ugly head again and compound your next one with issues from within your old grief you didn't deal with fully the first time. There are no rules or patterns for how it will play out.

Letting go of expectations is not easy, but I can tell you what one of the big keys for me was, forgiving myself. Now, I'm not referring to the irrational guilt many of us feel when someone close dies unexpectedly. Dealing with that guilt and forgiving yourself is one of the possible stages you may go through. What I'm talking about is forgiving yourself for the little things you may do during the day while you are grieving. Yelling at the guy behind the counter in 7-11, being rude to someone who is offering you a helping hand, pushing your pet away just because you can't stand to have anything close to you at that moment; all these things can eat at you because you "shouldn't" be acting that way. But I'm here to tell you, "It's okay, you are grieving." Many of us reflect back on our days after the fact and beat ourselves up for being harsh with others. It's okay. It happens. You are grieving. If it makes you feel better, go back to that person and apologize later, but don't let the expectation that you will not take the anger and hurt you feel out on others make you beat yourself up even more. It happens. It's normal.

Of course there are more than just the "should" expectations you and others will put on yourself. There are expectations of how events and future days will progress, like holidays and birthdays. For those of us grieving the loss of a dear one at those times, it's expectations of what might happen that can be the most horrible thing to deal with.

Take Christmas for instance. From the first jingle bell I hear, the holidays take on the countenance of the Polar Express bearing down on me like a massive steel beast of sadness and depression that is inescapable as I'm bound helplessly by tinsel and bows to the tracks of despair. It seems that everything I see, smell and hear brings back the memories of celebrations gone by filled with laughter and joy, and the loved boy who is so glaringly absent from the current holiday planning. But I have discovered that it is in fact these expectations that prove to be the worst of it. The weeks of dreading the holiday's arrival grow more and more intense. The days leading up to the big celebration become filled with mood swings and excessive indulgence in destructive yet comforting behaviors like overeating or binge drinking. The onslaught of holiday parties makes this easy. It's safe to say that if you look around at the revelers at your next big holiday gathering, the person who is the loudest caroler and seemingly full of the most enthusiastic holiday cheer may in fact just be working the hardest at warding off the most horrible of Ghosts of Christmases Past.

What has surprised me the most during the Christmases since David's death is that on the actual day the horrible bouts of paralyzing tears and anger tend to never materialize. Perhaps it is because the days preceding have been so full of angst and sorrow that by the time the holiday actually arrives my grief engine is running on empty. Or possibly, it's simply the same as such infinitesimally less dreaded events like a shot from the doctor or visit to the dentist; they just never prove to be as horrible as imagined. More often than not, the actual holiday tends to be a relatively "good" day, especially in comparison to the prelude.

That's not to say that there are not tears. No, there is always a moment when the emptiness finds a place to express itself. But I have found more often than not, just as with tears of grief, holiday tears tend to be healing tears, and full of love. The tears on holidays are shed from beautiful memories of days gone by. These memories are good memories, full of warmth and tenderness. And though the tears are born of longing, they represent the entire reason the holidays exist. Love. Family. Giving. They remind me that in the not too distant past I was blessed with wonderful riches, and they hold the promise that life moves forward.

I have found that to help combat these "special day" expectations doing things which were passed down from my parents and on back can be an important part of a successful holiday. Decorating the tree and house. Putting up holiday lights. They all bring back memories of my boy. And though the very first time I did these things it was difficult, it has been important to my healing. Just as we cannot avoid experiencing grief if we plan to move forward, these traditions performed in the days before a holiday help me stay in touch with my boy. And they also give me things to do so I don't dwell on the expectations. The tears are turning to laughter as the years progress, and hanging ornaments that had meaning to him, and carrying on old traditions, gives me connection not only to future generations, but also to my past that is no longer physically present.

I'm not telling you what you should do, I certainly don't want to force any new expectations on you. I'm simply sharing what has worked for me in combating these "special day" expectations.

When you are grieving any type of expectation can derail your journey of healing. The best thing to do is to learn to let them all go. It's much easier said then done, but if you can learn to just live in the now when you feel the expectations coming on, and stop looking ahead or trying to do what you or others think you should do, then you can minimize the destructive effects expectations can wreak on your life. Replace the "should be"s others offer with some other well worn platitudes; "Roll with it" "Take it as it comes'" "Cross that bridge when you get to it," and not at all the least of them, "Improvise."

See what I did there? Yes that's right, "improvise." As you'll soon see, it's another of the positive side effects of Healing Improv Workshops, learning to live in the here and now, and not trying to guess what's coming. Just deal with what's right in front of you. Which brings us to the next chapter…

IMPROV SAVED ME

    Four weeks after David died the funeral was over, the relatives had gone home, and I had cried so many tears I had to keep drinking Gatorade to keep from passing out from dehydration. It was time to try and get back to life. As an actor and a teacher of improv comedy, that meant going back to my classes, and back to the stage to make people laugh on Saturday night. No easy task.

    My boss and director of the improv companies had more than understood, being the father of kids himself. We had often compared notes of our sons' exploits on the sports fields. The fact my son had died while playing football was not lost on him. He had told me I could take whatever kind of time I needed.

    I wasn't sure as I made the drive down into Los Angeles that night to perform, whether or not I was going to be able to do it. I certainly wasn't doing myself any good sitting home stewing in my grief, but getting on stage, finding the focus to put my pain aside and make jokes about Brittany Spears, or Rush Limbaugh seemed both inconceivable and perhaps even downright disrespectful to my boy. But my best friend was in the troupe of actors, and I loved all of these folks dearly. Most of them had traveled out to be at our son's funeral to pay their respects and support Leslie, Abby and I, so I felt they would have my back. If things went horribly wrong and I was suddenly reduced to a whimpering puddle of tears on the stage, I knew they would understand and be there for me.

As my SUV crossed over the hill down into the Valley I popped in the CD of music from my boy's memorial service I had put together, and proceed to drive the next 15 miles with tears streaming down my face. Navigating the freeways in Los Angeles is never simple, but I do not recommend it when under the severe influence of grief. I probably made all the drunk and stoned (it is LA) drivers on the road look like Jeff Gordon (my son's favorite NASCAR driver) by comparison.

By some miracle, I made it to the theater. When I arrived another troupe about to go onstage gave me huge hugs of support and love, and my cast was there ready to warm-up for our time on stage. We sat around and talked for an hour or so. There was some laughter, and tears, and as time came for us to get ready to take the stage, I felt like maybe this was the wrong decision. But I wasn't going to tell them that. I had to get back to living. "Yeah that's right, get back to living." I whispered to myself several times. We did our warm-ups and we were ready to go. I had 5 minutes.

I walked out into the alley behind theater and looked up to the star filled night (or at least as starred filled as LA skies get). I asked my son, "Is this okay?" "Do you understand me being back here so soon?" I had already come to the painful revelation we all have after we lose someone so important; "The world goes on turning no matter what has occurred." But that didn't necessarily mean I was ready to join in. I looked up for some kind of sign, even though I don't really believe in that kind of thing. I stood there staring into the void, struggling to hear his voice tell me, "It's okay Dad." But all I could hear was the traffic out on Ventura Blvd. and the noises of life around me. After another wave of tears threatened to overtake me, I turned back to go inside.

Now, I have already stated that I don't believe in "signs" and the like, but as I walked back into the theater I looked up one last time. There, brighter than any of the stars shining down, a shooting star suddenly streaked across the sky and fell, as if it was aimed, at the theater. I stopped in my tracks. I looked around, had anyone else seen that? Nope, only me.

We huddled together in the small dressing room filled with dirty costumes that had been thrown on hundreds of times by improv actors looking for a quick character. We linked arms and the cast sent all the positive energy they had to me. I was still thinking about the shooting star.

The pre-show music started and out my best friend went to welcome the audience. Moments later, I was charging onto the stage with the other 7 players, clapping and feigning excitement.

I can't tell you what I did that night on stage. I know there were laughs, and it felt good to get that nourishment from strangers, which I have always craved. But something else happened. Something wonderful. In the 90 minutes I was on stage doing improv, I was released from the grief that had been hounding me. It didn't go away for good, as soon as the show was over, it came back. But for those 90 minutes, being in the moment, listening to the others on stage and reacting, the art of improv demanded that I not think of anything outside of where we were. I had nowhere else to be, and nothing else to do. For those brief 90 minutes, I got a vacation from my grief.

For the next year, those Saturday night shows were a salvation. I had a place I could go to escape the all-encompassing grief, and be me. Not only that, it kept my emotional gates open. I was flexing my emotional muscles. Laughter, much like sobbing, is an involuntary reaction. Any kind of emotional reaction helps keep your soul open, and allows you to direct the stifling heartache when it comes, so that it can be useful. When the tears came, it began to have the same effect as a summer thunderstorm that clears away the oppressive humidity, removing the burdensome sadness and leaving me feeling "refreshed." It's one of the reasons I have started the non-profit charity HEALING IMPROV, to help others who feel stuck in their grief through Comedy Improv Grief Workshops.

Improv Comedy saved my life.

HEALING IMPROV

"Because when you're laughing, there is no other emotion in that moment except for joy."
~Robert Schimmel

    Like I said, in the year after David died, the fact I had somewhere to go to perform and teach improv comedy saved me. I mean this quite literally. Going to the show every week, getting on stage, and making others laugh gave relief from the overwhelming grief that had a stranglehold on my life. It also kept me laughing. If there is one thing I have learned performing improv and sketch comedy it is that if you are having fun on stage, chances are the audience is too. The people in my improv troupe in Los Angeles were a wacky, crazy group of immature people who were as neurotic, insecure and conceited as the day is long. In other words, they were my kind of people. Show people. Actors. And as such they were brimming with creativity and life. This energy was always infectious. No matter what kind of mood I might be in when I arrived at the theater for warm-ups, that mood was bound to improve. These people were my friends. Not the kind of friends that you might share the intimate details of your life with, but like spirits who understood I was an eccentric soul who thrived on not taking life too seriously and making fun of those that do.

When my family and I decided to relocate to Michigan, I was apprehensive that I would be able to find the kind of free spirited people that I had surrounded myself with for the last twenty five plus years. It didn't take me long to dive into the theater scene in Michigan to find out. Turns out there are wacky, crazy immature people who are as neurotic, insecure and conceited as the day is long in the Midwest too. The only difference in Michigan was that these unique people are, for the most part, not driven to become famous for their neurosis like the actors in LA looking for their big break. The people in Michigan work long hours and get on stage for the love of performing and sharing their love with others in the community. It suited my state of mind well. I met with the powers that be at the local community theatre, one of the largest in the country, and expressed not only my desires to perform, but also that I thought perhaps I could lend my teaching expertise to their theatre school, which is also one of the finest community theatre schools in the country. They embraced my enthusiasm and experience and quickly put me to work teaching an adult improvisation class. It was during this class that the idea of using what I had spent my life doing could help others who are experiencing grief in their lives.

The class I was given to teach was full of people who had much less experience on stage than the average "beginner" in improv classes in Los Angeles. In fact most of them were performing novices. There were a few retirees, a few middle aged people who were looking to learn something new, and several college aged people who either had done a little improv or had always wanted to try it because friends told them they were funny. What I discovered was that the improvisational exercises I was teaching them were having a profound effect on all of them. Not being experienced performers, most of them were not very comfortable at the start getting up in front of everyone, but that changed quickly. As the weeks passed I noticed there was a zeal amongst them to attend class growing very quickly. This wide spectrum of people were becoming fast friends, enjoying the eclectic mix and building teamwork with each other; a true camaraderie for them all to excel at the work. Unlike the students in Los Angeles, who mostly were focused on building a skill they could parade in front of casting directors, these students were building a small community amongst themselves that was exciting and bridged any differences they may have had before they came to class. I approached the powers that be at the theatre to institute a new training program in their school that would focus on improv and eventually form an improv troupe to perform under the banner of the theatre.

They liked the idea. They also liked the possibility I suggested that this troupe could also do corporate training for companies and expand the reach of the theatre into the community at large. This would not only bring in money directly from fees charged for the training, but also aid the theatre in its goal to attract corporate donations, an important part of any community theatre's survival. It was at this juncture that the executive director of the theatre invited me to attend the upcoming board of directors meeting and share some improv with the board. He said that normally they hire a musician to provide music during the meeting, but that it might be fun to "shake things" up a bit and introduce something new to the board that, though they sit on the board of directors of a large theatre organization, have little performance experience themselves. I loved the idea. I realized that to some extent it was an audition to show him that I had the abilities to do what I had professed I could with corporate training, but I also welcomed the chance to directly get the board excited about what I was bringing to the theatre community.

The evening was a rousing success. The board members got up, and though many joked about how they weren't performers by any means, the exercises did what they have always done; got a lot of people, more used to being reserved and conservative, laughing and joking at themselves, building camaraderie and opening communication between them in ways it had not been established before. And all in about 40 minutes!

During my discussion with the theatre I had casually mentioned that improv might even be an effective tool to help people deal with grief. The associate director had expressed how wonderful that idea sounded to her. I sort of laughed it off, but it stuck in my head and started to grow. After the class had been completed, and I had engaged the board of directors, I was home one evening watching a documentary on Mel Brooks. Mel has always been a hero of mine, not only is he a brilliant well educated man, but his comedy appeals to the very basic element in all of us. At one point in the documentary, Susan Stroman, Tony Award winning Broadway director and choreographer, spoke about her experiences with grief. Her husband Mike Ockrent was to have been the director of MEL BROOKS' THE PRODUCERS on Broadway, but he became ill and died before the show took shape. Mel Brooks pursued Susan, who up until then had not directed on Broadway, to take the reins and be not only the choreographer, but the director as well. She told him she didn't think she could do it; the grief was too strong. Mel Brooks begged her to do it, not only for the show, but also for her own wellbeing. He told her, "You can cry before you come to work, and cry when you get home, but during the day at the theater, I promise you we will laugh and live, and it will give you new life." She trusted him, and took the job. Today she says that her relationship with Mel Brooks was the strongest she has ever experienced in the theater, and credits him with saving her from overpowering grief.

Suddenly Healing Improv exploded into full vision in my mind. All the years I had spent learning to guide people through improv had a purpose. All the time spent learning games that connected people in ways they never expected, all while making them laugh and have a good time, suddenly came together. Though there is nothing in the world that would ever bring my boy back to me, here was something he would have LOVED. A chance to take the most horrible thing that had ever happened to me and apply the work I had spent my life building to help others suffering from the same unthinkable pain we had survived. Improv and performing, the one thing other then my family I have ever truly been passionate about, now took on an entirely different purpose. Of course, as I told Abby as all the pieces to bring aid to those suffering fell into place, the most difficult thing now was to actually do it.

So what exactly is Healing Improv?

Healing Improv is an interactive workshop of improvisational exercises for people dealing with grief from the death of a loved one, or medical situations in their life or the life of a loved one, who feel overwhelmed by circumstances and are having trouble moving forward in their lives. That's the long description. The short description is it's fun comedy improv games to help you learn to laugh again.

The exercises and games used in Healing Improv are not groundbreakingly new. They have been used and taught in different variations for many years. Though improvisation has been around basically since people first started telling stories of the day's hunt around the tribal fire, the first person really credited with putting it into a structured technique is Viola Spolin. Interestingly, much of what she pioneered which became the backbone of improvisational groups like The Second City, The Groundlings, and just about every other improv troupe out there, came from her early experiences in social work. She was inspired by techniques and games being used by Neva Boyd to help bridge cultural differences and reach people of different ethnic backgrounds through art, dance, music and role-playing. Ms. Spolin realized these techniques could reach a wide diversity of people, and much of her early work was focused on children and reaching them through her improvisational games.

One of the keys to Healing Improv's success is this connection to the ability of people to let go of the social norms and constraints that the adult world has put on them.

These games and exercises reach people on a playful level, and enable them to reconnect with their youthful spirit, which is not afraid to laugh, cry and express it's emotions freely. All too often people suffering from grief and depression are told to "get over it," or "move on." Those who are suffering in their pain are told, if not directly, at least by implication, that their pain is not acceptable in the grown-up world and they need to get past it. The truth is we never "get over it." It's absurd that our society treats grief and heartache in this manner, when grief over the loss of a loved one is something that happens to almost everyone at one time or another. The key is learning to recognize the pain and find a way to integrate it into our lives where we understand it, and can accept its existence and direct it into a positive influence in our lives, not a destructive one. The games I describe here are useful tools in achieving these ends. Through creativity and participation, the games free the participants to let go of societal restraints in a safe environment. Simply put, it gives people the permission to act foolish and be free within a group of individuals who are going through similar emotional trials in their own lives.

When David died, what I found most comforting was to know that I was not alone. Knowing that there were others walking around and functioning in the world who had experienced what I was going through gave me hope and comfort. If they had found a way to move forward and live life, not simply survive…even thrive in the face of devastating loss, then perhaps I could as well. Often the misplaced guilt we experience after someone dies makes us feel we don't deserve to laugh and enjoy ourselves. Healing Improv sessions assemble people who are traveling down similar emotional paths. When led into the exercises and games by an enthusiastic leader, participants feel comfortable to allow themselves to laugh and release feelings that society outside the walls of the group may not, because they are surrounded by those who understand. This is why each workshop begins with a time of sharing so that everyone knows they are in the company of others living the same challenges they are. Once the sharing is complete, we come together to play. It also, by its nature, forces people to listen and communicate with others about subjects not related to their loss or heartache. This human connection is integral in getting people reconnected with the world around them.

Many of these games have been used in corporate training, or other team building environments. Communication, understanding of other's perspectives, and appreciation of other's talents are all major benefits of corporate training through improvisation. These three elements are all major components to how improv helps those in grief as well. Again it's the human interaction, the challenge to stay focused on the group and the game's goals that allow people to experience spontaneous joy, and freeing interaction.

The final element of what makes the workshops so helpful is what is best described as constructive avoidance. Millions of Americans turn to alcohol, or drugs, both illegal and those prescribed by doctors, to avoid the painful ramifications of grief. They take these drugs to dull the pain, and make it less severe. They use the drugs to get a break from the overwhelming heartache. I had many people tell me after David died that going to the doctor to get "something to take the edge off" was completely acceptable. I pass no judgment on those that do, but the problem with drugs and alcohol is that while sufferers are avoiding the emotional strife, they are not doing anything constructive to help heal their spirit. Don't misunderstand me; I would love to be able to tell you that I faced David's death with pure strength and valor. That I stared grief and heartbreak squarely in the eye and by the mere potency of my character and magnitude of my moral fiber, I caused it to retreat back to the dirty ugly little corner it crawled out of, never to be seen again. But that would be disingenuous. I had my indulgences that helped me dull the pain, mine most frequently coming in the shape of a pizza, but I was not completely devoid of my dalliances.

The problem with all these assisted means of avoidance are that not only does nothing constructive happen during the use of these measures, but afterwards the users are often left with a dependency on them, and a need to use them more often and in greater quantities because they have not used them to repair, but simply to temporarily escape. Healing Improv workshops provide the same escape from distress by engaging the participants' minds in an activity that requires them to use their heads to stay occupied with the games at hand. It removes the pain and heartache in a similar fashion to artificial means, but in doing so it increases human interaction, humor and connectivity. These results are supportive to healing and moving forward. The physical exertion helps relieve stress as well and allows the body to let go of tension. I must admit as an over 25-year practitioner, improv comedy can be very "addictive," but I mean that in the best possible sense of the word. Improv is not addictive in a physical way; it just simply is so much damned fun you want to do it over and over again.

One last thought. Sometimes when people hear "comedy improv" they are hesitant to participate because they fear being "on stage." They protest that they are not funny and have no interest in trying to make other people laugh. But that's not what Healing Improv workshops are about. There is no stage at Healing Improv workshops. No one is watching and judging. Everyone is participating. It's not a performance environment; it's a play environment. The only person you are charged with entertaining during a workshop is yourself.

THE 1ST WORKSHOP

"We can't help everyone, but everyone can help someone."
~Ronald Reagan

  Even though I have been teaching others improvisation for over 25 years, I have to admit I was a bit apprehensive before our first Healing Improv Grief Workshop. I had been careful not to bill myself or what we were doing with HI as anything more than what it was: a comedy improv workshop that would be centered around people who were grieving and helping them laugh and connect with others. I knew I could handle the laugh and connection part. Improv games, when played properly and enthusiastically, are as close to a sure thing as there is when it comes to those two results. I knew from years of experience that I had a knack for getting people involved and excited about standing amongst a group of strangers acting like an idiot and forgetting their self-consciousness. This, of course, is primarily assured by the fact that I have no shame when it comes to making a fool of myself. A self-deprecating attitude and energetic delivery go a long way in convincing others that it's okay to let their "grown-up" guard down and join in on the fun.

  The part that had me a bit apprehensive was the grief part. After all, this first session was happening on the 4th anniversary of David's death. I am still very much in the process of traversing the obstacle course of grief myself. The day before the workshop, I spent a great deal of my morning "clearing out" the tears and emotions that reside just under the surface of my seemingly together life. I knew that, just like every year since David's death, this day was going to be the kind of day where I was likely to snap at people and pets that didn't deserve it. I knew that the wrong song on the radio at the wrong time might send me down an emotional trail that would lead to uncontrollable tears. So, the day before the workshop I got proactive about it and went in search of the waterworks. They did not disappoint. I posted some pictures online of David and the family, reread a few favorite quotes, and then shared a few thoughts openly online, and as the tears came I did what I have learned to do when I have the luxury, I leaned into them.

So, having flushed the obvious heartache in a healthy way, I figured I was prepared to walk into a room of strangers and guide them down the same road I was so familiar with. I made sure that the workshop room would be prepared for what we might encounter. I bought adhesive nametags so everyone could feel at ease and know people's names if they so chose. I bought no less than 6 boxes of tissues and strategically set them about the room so a box would never be more than a few steps away if the need arose (and it did). Leslie and Abby had baked cookies the night before in abundance so that there would be some "comfort food" if someone (possibly me) felt the need to feed their grief with something tasty and familiar. Of course, it dawned on me halfway through the evening that the chocolate chip cookies were fine, but the peanut butter kiss could have been a disastrously bad idea, the last thing we needed was to have someone go into anaphylactic shock from a peanut allergy. Thank goodness they didn't. I also had small water bottles in case anyone needed to replenish bodily fluids after a crying jag. I even thought ahead to napkins, small plates and individually packaged mints, just in case someone wanted to make sure they didn't have grief breath (I made that term up, it means nothing). Brochures? Check. Donation jar, with neat professional label and pre filled with a few dollars to give people the right idea? Check. Music? Check. I chose the lovely soundtrack to "Somewhere in Time," a sweet uplifting yet slightly yearning melody that I felt captured the mood perfectly for the "pre-show." Signup sheet so I could email people afterwards? Check. Everything was how it needed to be.

I still was nervous.

As people started to arrive, there was a friendly understanding nature to everyone. We all knew why we were there, and all assumed that the other people in attendance were also struggling with some kind of grief, most likely over the loss of a loved one. What surprised me a bit, and of course it made perfect sense, was that most of the people were older than I was. I say it made sense because as we get older in life the chances of us having lost someone that would bring us grief increases just by the mere number of years and number of people we've met. Once we felt we had most of the folks present, we got started. I was comforted that one of our Healing Improv Board of Directors, a pastor at a local church, a fellow actor and like spirit whose stepson had died the year before David, was also there. I figured if anybody really lost himself or herself in grief, he would have some experience in lending assistance.

We all sat on the upholstered hassocks I had arranged in a circle at one end of the room, and I dove in. Leslie had decided not to attend. Partly is was due to the fact that we are still in different places on our grief journey, and she was not sure she was ready to be there, and partially because it was the 4th anniversary of David's death and she didn't want to leave Abby with a baby sitter or friend on this night. Oh, who am I kidding? Leslie wanted to be with Abby. I don't blame her. There had been more than a few moments in the last week that I had questioned the sanity of what had initially seemed like such a good idea, to do this on this date. But I was here now. The months of hard work raising funds, organizing games, doing TV, radio and newspaper interviews to get the word out, had led to these people sitting here looking to me to help ease their sadness. So I did what has become a very natural and healing thing for me to do in the last 4 years; I talked about David. I gave them all the Readers Digest version of what had happened to our boy. I spoke of how the games we were going to play had helped keep me sane after his death. I told them that for years I had joked about how I performed comedy improv because it was better than therapy, and ironically I had discovered that my joke had proven to be true in my life. And then I turned to the person on my left and passed the buck to them to tell their tale of woe.

For the next 45 minutes we made our way slowly around the circle of wounded hearts, telling everyone our pain and sadness. The group was very supportive of each other. Some voiced the concern that their grief was not as bad as other folks in the room, but everyone assured them that it wasn't healthy to compare their problems with anyone else's. The truth was, we had all felt the need to come to this place and share with others our pain in hopes that this strange thing called Healing Improv might provide us some relief from our burdensome heartache. If you felt moved to be here, you had a right to tell your story. Some people had pain from a loss that was old and had resurfaced or compounded recently. Some people had pain from a recent serious illness diagnosis and were angry and hurt by the news, and felt disconnected. Some had recent losses, within the past year, and were reaching out to different avenues of healing to find their way forward. We all sat and listened, tears were shed, some laughs were shared, and frustration spilled out. After we had made it all the way around the circle, I made a few more comments to reassure all that we were here to travel forward, and then urged them to get up on their feet and join me in the open space of the room.

There was some apprehension in the room, but everyone was resigned to the fact that here they were, they had signed up for this oxymoronic "Comedy Improv Grief Therapy" and there was no turning back now.

    I asked them to form a big circle and explained a tried and true game of movement and labels that tends to get silly and funny as it becomes more challenging. A few people were resistant to fully commit to the activity, but not seriously so. A few tried to fade back out of the circle in the first few rounds, but I humorously goaded them to stay with us and rejoin the group, and they did. Soon there was laughter and excitement filling the space. People were truly enjoying themselves. We moved on to another game and the group, less hesitant, but now wary of a new game, grumbled a little at the new challenge, but dove in anyway. We laughed and started joking with each other, laughing at our own foibles and missteps. There was connection happening here.

    We took a break to allow everyone to get a drink of water and enjoy some of Leslie and Abby's delicious cookies. There was animated conversation happening now. People were really starting to connect. I looked over the plethora of games I decided I could play with a group, and picked three more that would suit the age and attitudes we had in the room best. We embarked on the second half of our journey together, and the connections kept flourishing, and laughter continued. By the time the final game ended, a singing game where everyone takes turns in the middle of the circle singing songs in a stream of consciousness manner, there was an audible sigh of disappointment that our time was coming to a close. A few turned to look at the clock, surprised at the way the time had flown by. I thanked them all for being strong and brave and enthusiastic participants, and told them that they had helped me a great deal, and if they had gotten out of the evening even half of what I had, then it was a huge success. People asked for extra brochures to share with their church groups. Others exchanged phone numbers. I got a few hugs and kisses as thanks. I was on cloud nine. Early on during our sharing time a few of the people present had revealed that they themselves were therapists, or had been therapists, and had always thought that humor would be a great tool, which is why they had sought the workshop out. They too were very thankful and positive about what we had done.

I left the evening greatly gratified and humbled that I was able to help others. What we did does not seem all that difficult to me, but then again I have always thrived on eliciting laughter from people and refused to grow up years ago. The playing of games and making an ass of myself has always come naturally, but for many, especially those struggling, that is not the case. I find myself excited to share these Healing Improv Grief Workshops with so many other people, who are struggling in so many different ways. Next month we get to do another adult workshop, and add a workshop for young people aged 12-17.

I have found a calling. And much like he did when I got him up around the bonfire with our friends and made him do some improv games with everybody while we were camping, David is somewhere laughing like a loon at the silliness, camaraderie and teamwork of everyone at the workshops. He's loving it. And so am I.

FINAL THOUGHTS

Thank you for letting me share with you the tragic tale of losing my son David and the journey my family continues to travel in dealing with that loss. You have read that my experiences teaching and performing improv helped keep me sane in the aftermath of his death. You've read why Healing Improv works, and you've read about the first Healing Improv Comedy Grief Workshop. All that's left is to give you a sampling of some of the games used in the workshops to help those who are struggling with their grief. As I have said, these games are not new per se; versions have been around for many years, used as teaching tools for performers learning improv, and in corporate training situations to build communication and teamwork in the business world. I have put my own spin on some of them, and some of them are just as I learned them during my last quarter century of improv experience.

I am not a physiologist or doctor, I am an improviser. The thoughts and techniques I share here do not come from a textbook or a learned study of grief and emotional issues at a university. They come from having lived and survived the worst experience of my life. I stumbled across the fact that this fun I have been playing at for years can bring some comfort and healing to people suffering with grief. The improv games are not intended to be a one stop "cure," because grief is not a disease that can be cured. Rather, they should be looked on as a course of treatment for one of the most difficult challenges we all face at some point in our lives. It is my sincere wish that they help ease the pain and anguish in people's lives. They are not a substitute for counseling and therapy, but rather an additional tool to help clear the fog and misery of pain and loss. I want to assure you, if I can find the way forward, you can too. There is life to live, joy to be experienced, and a future to be explored. I wish you the very best of fortunes in your journey.

Peace, Light and Laughter,
Bart Sumner - www.Healing-Improv.org

APPENDIX

HEALING IMPROV GAMES

> *"Man is most nearly himself when he achieves the seriousness of a child at play."*
>
> ~Heraclitus - Greek Philosopher 535–475 BC

There really are no wrong ways to do these improv games. It's important to understand what the "rules" of each game are and to try and follow them to get the maximum benefit from each game, but the structures are loose and having fun is the only necessity. Take a few moments to look and see what the Goals and Keys to Success are for each game so that you have an idea of what can be gained from each exercise. It always helps to know what you are shooting for with a group.

It is always helpful to have an experienced improviser lead the games because there is often a common hesitance among the general population to drop all conventions of being a "Grown-up" and to allow oneself to participate openly. Someone with improv experience knows what it takes to loosen a group up and encourage participants to let their guards down and join in the fun. But anyone who is open, caring, enthusiastic and willing to laugh at himself or herself can lead a group through these games.

The structures are meant to be played in an open, well-lit area where there is ample room to move about and interact. After each game applaud the participants and encourage them to applaud each other and themselves. Some of the games are quite difficult to actually do without making mistakes, and that's a designed part of the fun and should be used as an opportunity to laugh at ourselves. Remember, it's all about the fun, there is no right answer; there is simply play.

Good luck and enjoy.

NICE TO MEET YOU

NICE TO MEET YOU (5 or more participants) is an icebreaker game designed to have everyone make contact with the rest of the participants and ignite the energy of camaraderie and fun.

HOW TO PLAY:

    Have the Participants stand in a group in the center of the space. Instruct them on your mark to begin moving around the group heartily greeting the other participants by shaking hands, with either hand, and declaring "Nice To Meet You." The one rule of the game is that they cannot stop shaking hands with one person to greet another until they physically make contact with the next person. This way the entire group is continuously connected and must begin to work together so that no individual is left disconnected from the group, without a connection, at any time.

VARIATIONS:
- Give the group different conditions that apply by suggesting variations on the greeting:
    "You are in a German Drinking Hall"
    "You are in a church that demands hushed voices"
    "You are in a Wild West saloon"
    "You must sing your greetings to each other"
    "You can't talk, but must make animal noises"
    "You are in outer-space"
    "Use a made up language"
- Any other variation which changes the volume, speed or demeanor of the greetings is acceptable.

GOALS & KEYS TO SUCCESS:
Energy.
Movement.
Connection.
Familiarity.

Make sure the participants stay connected and do not leave anyone without a connection.

NAME MOTIONS

NAME MOTIONS (6-20 participants) is a word and motion game encouraging participation and getting to know each other.

HOW TO PLAY:
> The group stands in a large circle facing in. One participant says their name accompanied by a simple movement for each syllable of their name. The next participant repeats the first participant's name and motions and then does their own name and unique motion. Participant 3 has to do the first 2 names and motions and then add his own, and so on, and so on, until the final participant has to do everyone's name and movements, and his own. It should then continue around the circle once so that everyone has to do everyone's name and motion as well.

VARIATIONS:
> • Make participants sing their names and do a little dance step with it.

GOAL & KEYS TO SUCCESS:
> Learning everyone's name.
> Energy.
> Laughter.
> Teamwork.

LION-DOG-MOUSE

LION-DOG-MOUSE (8-25 participants) is a sound/action game designed to get the group to work together and be silly.

HOW TO PLAY:
Participants stand in a circle facing each other. Explain to the group that on "Go" in the count "One, Two, Three, GO!" they must do one of only three things:
1) "Roar" loudly like a LION and make a clawing motion with their hands.
2) "Woof" loudly like a DOG and put their hands up on their heads like dog-ears.
3) "Squeak" loudly like a MOUSE and put their hands in front of their nose like tiny mouse paws.

Of course on the first turn you will have some Lions, some Dogs and some Mice. You then repeat the same process, informing the group that the idea is to get them all to agree on the same animal, Lion, Dog or Mouse, and you will continue to repeat the process until they all agree on the same animal. Make sure there is no discussion ahead of time between the participants, and that everyone does their animal at the same time on your command "Go."

VARIATIONS:
• Do the same game, but make the participants turn around so they face outward.
•Do the same game but make everyone close his or her eyes.
• Do the same game but tell everyone they cannot do the same animal twice (this will make it very difficult, and the laughter from frustration will grow as they try)

GOAL & KEYS TO SUCCESS:
Working together.
Movement.
Sound.
Silliness.
Perseverance.
Laughter.

SUPER HERO CIRCLE

SUPER HERO CIRCLE (6-25 participants) is a sound & action game designed to get the group to interact together and be silly.

HOW TO PLAY:
 ROUND ONE-
One participant steps forward declaring a made-up Super Hero name (example - "Cheese Man") and makes a gesture to go along with that name. They step back into their place, and then the rest of the group steps forward and in unison, copies the name and gesture as closely as possible, and then steps back into their places.

The next participant in the circle steps forward and declares a different made-up Super Hero name, making a unique gesture to go along with that name. Again, the rest of the group steps forward, and in unison, copies that name and gesture as closely as possible.

Continue around the circle, having everyone declare his or her own unique made-up Super Hero name and gesture, and having the group copy it in unison.

Once the entire circle has gone, go around the circle a second time, with everyone keeping the same Super Hero name and gesture they did the first time, so that everyone gets to hear everyone's Super Hero character and gesture a second time to help them remember it.
(Continued)

 ROUND TWO-
One participant steps forward and does their Super Hero name and gesture, followed by "Tagging" someone else in the circle by doing their Super Hero name and gesture, and

then steps back into their place in the circle. The participant who was "Tagged" steps forward and repeats their own Super Hero name and gesture, doing it the right way in case the other participant didn't do it exactly right. Then that participant "Tags" another participant by doing another participant's Super Hero name and gesture. The group continues passing the Super Hero names and gestures around the group one at a time.

VARIATIONS:
- As the group gets more comfortable, speed up the "Tagging" making the game move faster and faster and faster.
- Start 2 Tagging chains at once, and challenge the group to keep both going, and then make that go faster and faster. If the same person gets his Super Hero called by both chains at the same time they simply do their own and do another's, and then do their own again and do a second one.
- With large groups of 15 or more you can try 3 at a time, expect it to go badly. LOL
- Use different categories other than "Super Hero." Examples: "Favorite Food" - "Favorite Sport" (Real or Made-up) – "Movie Title" – "Pet Peeve"
- FOR YOUNGER CHILDREN or as another variation use an animal name followed by a gesture and animal sound.

GOAL & KEYS TO SUCCESS:
Energy.
Concentration.
Movement.
Laughter.

These are Super Heroes, so the names should be loud and dramatic.

Make sure the gestures are big and distinct from the other players.

Silly names should be encouraged.

Laughter will happen, but as you speed the game up, encourage the group to focus in and LISTEN carefully so no one misses their character being used.

START A MOVEMENT AND PASS IT ON

START A MOVEMENT AND PASS IT ON (5-25 participants) is a sound/action game designed to get the group to work together, concentrate on their own "job" and be laugh at the difficulty of a seemingly simple task.

HOW TO PLAY:
    ROUND ONE:
    The group stands in a large circle facing each other. They begin to chant the following statement: "Start a movement and pass it on," in a metered four-count rhythm. Once the group has gotten into a steady rhythm repeating the phrase, one person starts a simple movement that is no longer than the four-count chant they are repeating. The participant to the left of that person joins in, doing the exact same motion on the second refrain of the four-count chant. With each successive refrain another participant joins in, moving around the circle. Make sure that only one participant joins with each refrain of the chant so that the movement moves around the circle in a steady even pattern. When the last person in the circle joins in and does the same movement everyone else is now doing, then on the next refrain of the chant the participant that started the movement changes his movement to something completely different. With each successive refrain, the person to the left changes from the original movement to the new movement. Make sure no one anticipates or begins the new movement until it is their turn to do so. And then when the new movement has moved all the way around the circle, again the first participant changes the motion, and so on.
    ROUND TWO:
    Using the same set up and same chant of "Start a Movement and pass it on," this time the participant that starts the movement changes his movement with each refrain of

the chant. The person to his left repeats his movement one refrain after the first participant, copying each new movement with each new refrain, and so on and so on. This round each participant is doing a different motion with every refrain, and copying the motion passed to them with each refrain. This is very difficult. Remind the participants to just focus on the person to their right, and only worry about copying them with each new refrain.

VARIATIONS:
- There are no variations on this game, ROUND TWO is difficult enough without making it harder.

GOAL & KEYS TO SUCCESS:
Working together.
Movement.
Concentration.
Sound.
Acceptance.
Perseverance.
Laughter.

This game may take several attempts to get the participants to get the grasp of staying with one motion until it is their turn to change. If the circle gets confused or it gets messy, laugh and encourage everyone by reminding the participants this is not easy, and to try again.

In ROUND TWO if they continue to make errors, and they will, tell them they may very well not be able to accomplish the task, and that's completely acceptable. Let them know it's okay to laugh at how hard and seemingly impossible it is. Remind them again it's not about getting it right, it's about having fun! Of course if they are able to actually make it all around the circle successfully, praise them and let them know how very special they are!

ONE WORD FAIRYTALE

ONE WORD FAIRYTALE (5-25 participants) is a word game designed to have the group work together to tell a familiar story from beginning to end, one word at a time.

HOW TO PLAY:
Participants stand or sit in a circle facing each other. Get a suggestion from the group for a familiar fairytale or children's story they all are relatively familiar with. Starting with one person, the group goes around the circle, with each person using just one word at a time to tell the story together. Encourage short, simple, complete sentences. Make sure when the end of the story is reached that the group knows it's okay to end with "The" "End" or "And" "They" "Lived" "Happily" "Ever" "After."

VARIATIONS:
• Use a common fairytale, but have the group tell it as if it is happening in today's world instead of in the past.
• Have the group turn around so they face outward and can't see each other as easily and must listen more intently.
• Tell an original story. For this the leader will have to begin the story with a simple sentence like, "There once was a boy named Jimmy who went to the beach…" and then pass the story to the group to continue, one word at a time.

GOAL & KEYS TO SUCCESS:
Working together.
Eye contact.
Listening.
Laughter.

Connection.

Remind the participants to speak up and speak clearly so everyone can hear them.

Remind the group to keep the sentences short and to the point.

Remind them to keep the story moving.

It is completely acceptable for the leader to interject or even pause the story to clarify what has been said and help the group.

It also helps to remind the group to try to reach the end of the story.

After the story is complete, discuss with the group in a lighthearted manner the story they told and how it may have deviated from what might be considered the normal way the story is told.

RADIO DIAL

RADIO DIAL (6-25 participants) is a singing game designed to raise energy and encourage participation and open up creativity.

HOW TO PLAY:
      The group stands in a large circle facing in. Tell the participants to imagine they are riding in a car and the person next to them keeps changing channels on the radio, but every new song that comes up seems to be attached to the last song in some way. Either the lyrics are somehow connected, or the artist is the same, or the style is the same. One participant volunteers to go to the center and be "The Radio" by singing a song, any song. As soon as another participant in the outer circle thinks of another song, any song, inspired by the first song, they step forward, "Change the channel" by tagging the first participant out and start singing their song. This continues, as participants continue to "Change Channels" by tagging each other out and singing new songs in a stream of conscious-like manner. The only condition is to sing loud and have your song be inspired in some way by the song before.

GOAL & KEYS TO SUCCESS:
      Energy.
      Creativity.
      Laughter.
      Teamwork.

      Keep the song choices moving quickly; instruct the group not to let anyone get stuck in the center for too long.

Encourage participants to sing along with songs they know.

Singing the right lyrics is not important, but commitment and energy is; singing "la-la-la" or making up lyrics is okay if you don't know all the words.

The leader can encourage participation by joining in freely and often at first.

FOLLOW THE FLOCK

FOLLOW THE FLOCK (6-25 participants) is a sound/action game designed to get the group to work together and be silly.

HOW TO PLAY:
Participants form a long single file line. The group leader plays music and the "Flock" moves around the room following the participant at the front of the line, doing what he or she does, and imitating their movements and going where she or he goes. The group leader then changes the song, the first participant goes to the end of the line and the next participant in line becomes the leader of the "Flock."

VARIATIONS:
- The leader can also call out different scenarios to influence the "Flock", i.e. "It's very Cold," "It's raining," "It's very windy."

GOAL & KEYS TO SUCCESS:
Energy.
Movement.

It helps to have the music loaded into an MP3 player where you can switch to the next song quickly.

Try to use a very varied selection of music from new to old, fast to slow, rock to country, and make the songs contrast from song to song.

Remember, not all the participants will be equally able to move about the space, so remind the group to not do anything too physically demanding and assure all participants it's okay to only do what they are comfortable doing, it's not how well you do the movements, but that you are joining in the fun.

Even with a small group this game can be very tiring, so don't leave any one participant as leader for too long a time.

TEAM COUNT TO 20

TEAM COUNT TO 20 (6-25 participants) is a counting game designed to get the group to work together and laugh at themselves.

HOW TO PLAY:
   The group stands in a large circle facing each other. The group leader starts a steady rhythm at about one beat per second. The group's job is to simply count to 20 one number at a time, one number per beat, but each number can be said by only one member of the group at a time. If more than one group member says a number, or if no one says the next number on the beat, the group must begin back at "1." The counting cannot simply go around the circle, and if the group has to restart at "0," then on the next attempt a participant cannot say the same number he or she said in the last attempt. This is a very hard thing to accomplish, and gets harder with larger groups.

VARIATIONS:
   • Have the group turn so they are facing out and cannot make eye contact with each other.
   • Have the group close their eyes.

GOAL & KEYS TO SUCCESS:
   Listening.
   Working together.
   Communication

   It helps to use a metronome to keep the beat.

   This exercise often proves to be impossible, but it is doable.

   Celebrate every time the group goes further than they did the last time.

Make sure the group knows how hard it is and encourage laughter at the difficulty of the task.

BING BANG BONG

BING BANG BONG (6-25 participants) is a pattern game designed to get the group to work together and make connections with other participants.

HOW TO PLAY:
The group stands in a circle facing each other. One participant makes eye contact, points at another participant and says "Bing." That participant than makes eye contact and points at different participant and says "Bang." and that participant makes eye contact and points at another participant and says "Bong." This continues, always following the order of Bing, Bang, Bong, with the goal to speed it up and get a fast rhythm going with no hesitations.

VARIATIONS:
• After the group has mastered the simple game, have the participants pass the pattern around the circle without pointing but by using only eye contact and the word.
• Progress to the final challenge; passing the pattern around the circle without pointing AND without the speaking "Bing" "Bang" "Bong" aloud. Have the group start the non-pointing version, and once they established the patter the leader calls "silent." Using only eye contact the group continues to pass the pattern around the circle; keeping track to themselves which word they are on. After a short time the leader calls "Stop," and asks the group to see which word they think they are on.

GOAL & KEYS TO SUCCESS:
Listening.
Eye contact.

Communication.

Focus.

Working together.

The real key to this game is making sure the participants pass the pattern around the group clearly and with intention.

Do not rush the simple patter, especially when the pointing stops or in "silent" mode.

CATCHING FIRE

CATCHING FIRE (6-25 participants) is a movement and sound game designed to raise energy, encourage participation, and open up creativity and listening.

HOW TO PLAY:

The group moves about the space freely, walking in straight lines without making noises. If they encounter another participant they simply turn in an opposite direction and continue walking. On the leader's cue tell the group it is okay for someone, anyone, to make a small noise and a movement as they continue to walk, and that the noise and movement should then spread throughout the group, so that everyone eventually is making that noise and movement. After the sound and movement has spread throughout the entire group, another participant can change the noise and movement to a different sound and movement, and that change should slowly move throughout the entire group until all are doing that same sound and movement. Another Participant can then change the sound and movement.

GOAL & KEYS TO SUCCESS:

Energy.
Creativity.

Make sure a new sound and movement does not begin until the old one has spread through the group completely.

Instruct the group that if 2 different sounds and movements get started at the same time, the group must decide together which one will "Win."

FUZZY DUCKY

FUZZY DUCKY (6-25 participants) is a counting game designed to challenge the participants to stay focused and think on their feet.

HOW TO PLAY:
The group stands in a circle facing each other. The goal is to go around the circle, one number and participant at a time, counting from 1 up to 49. But for each number that contains a "3" (i.e. 3, 13, 23…etc.) or is a multiple of 3 (3,6,9,12…etc.) the participant must say "Fuzzy" instead of the number. If the number contains a "7" (i.e. 7, 17, 27…etc.) or is a multiple of 7 (7, 14, 21…etc.) they must say "Ducky" instead of the number. If the number contains both numbers, or is a multiple of both, or a combination on the two (i.e. 21, 27, 35, 37…etc.) they must say "Fuzzy Ducky" instead of the number.

VARIATIONS:
• The only real variation here is to challenge the group to count to 100 or more.

GOAL & KEYS TO SUCCESS:
Thinking ahead.
Focus.

It gets very difficult and confusing when the group reaches the 20's and 30's.

Challenge the group to get faster and to count in a steady rhythm.

MIMIC LINE

MIMIC LINE (6-25 participants) is a movement game that challenges participants to copy each other's movements and pass them on to the next participant.

HOW TO PLAY:
The group stands in a long single file line facing the same direction. The last participant in line taps the participant in front of him or her on the shoulder so that he or she turns to face them. The last participant does an elaborate yet short silent movement. After seeing the movement, the next to last participant turns back around and taps the next participant on the shoulder so he or she turns around. They then do the movement they saw as best as they can for that next participant to watch, who then turns and passes it on, and so on until the first participant in line finally gets to see the movement. Then you compare the movement the last participant saw, with what the first participant actually did.

VARIATIONS:
• Make the movements longer and more elaborate.

GOAL & KEYS TO SUCCESS:
Focus.

If the group is good at passing along the movement, make the movements longer and more challenging.

SHE SELLS SEASHELLS

SHE SELLS SEASHELLS (8-25 participants) is a word game that challenges participants to find word combinations that fit the game.

HOW TO PLAY:
    Group stands in a large circle facing in towards a participant designated as "The Caller." The Caller turns around with eyes closed until someone yells "Stop." The Caller points at the participant they are facing and calls out a letter of the alphabet. The participant must then create a statement that uses a person's name or type of animal, an item or service to sell, and a location, all beginning with the given letter before The Caller can count to 5.

   Example:

   "B" – "Bobby sells Balls in Boston"

   "K" – "Kangaroos sell Ketchup in Kazakhstan"

   If the participant does not do it successfully they become the Caller in the middle and the Caller takes their place in the circle.

   The Caller cannot repeat a letter that has been given to another participant.

VARIATIONS:
   • Change the type of statement being created to include types of cars, or song titles, or foods or types of clothing, etc.

GOAL & KEYS TO SUCCESS:
   Focus.

Spontaneity.
Creativity.
Energy.
Friendly Competition.

As Frustration builds make sure to keep the laughter flowing.

Encourage getting all the players a turn.

Reward creative uses even if the letters may not exactly fit the games rules.

CONDUCTED PET PEEVE SYMPHONY

CONDUCTED PET PEEVE SYMPHONY (8-25 participants) is a sound, word and movement game that challenges participants to open up emotionally and make loud noises and let go of self-conscious barriers.

HOW TO PLAY:
    The participants stand in a large circle facing in towards the "SYMPHONY CONDUCTOR." The Conductor goes around the circle and asks each participant to name a "Pet Peeve," or in other words, something that really makes him or her angry. It can be silly or serious, but it should be something people do that the participant can complain about. Example:
> "People that leave the toilet seat up,"
> "People that put an empty milk carton back in the fridge."

All participants should have their own unique pet peeve. The Conductor then tells his "Symphony" to warm up by complaining aloud about their Pet Peeve all at once. After all have "warmed up" he stops them and explains he will conduct the symphony by pointing to individuals, and when pointed to they should "rant" about their Pet Peeve. Explain that you may ask them to get louder or softer. Participants should stop "ranting" when you stop pointing at them, and others should begin when pointed at. Explain more than one person may be added to the group "ranting" and that they should pay attention and try to do whatever the conductor is asking for.

VARIATIONS:
- Conducted Symphonies can be done with lots of different topics:

Emotions
Animals Sounds
Different kinds of Laughs
Fake Foreign Languages
Types of Music
- Let participants take turns at being the conductor.

GOAL & KEYS TO SUCCESS:

Focus on the conductor.
Spontaneity.
Creativity.
Energy.

Following Directions

If a rhythm develops, stay with it.

Encourage lots of different levels.

Combine groups of "rants."

Get all participants going together.

An animated conductor encourages participation.

LIMERICKS

LIMERICKS (5-25 participants) is a word game where participants make up Limericks as a group, one line at a time.

<u>HOW TO PLAY</u>:
Participants stand in a circle facing each other. Explain to everyone the rhythm and rhyme scheme of Limericks.
A Limerick is a short 5-line poem, with an A-A-B-B-A rhyme scheme, where the first two lines and fifth line all rhyme with each other, and are a bit longer then the third and fourth lines. The third and fourth lines rhyme with each other but not the first, second and fifth.
Example:
A trapeze artist named Grace (A)
Did an act with her partner Pam Place (A)
Pam tried for a flip (B)
But suffered a slip (B)
And sadly poor Pam fell from Grace (A)

Begin by getting a suggestion from the group for a broad topic (i.e. cars, food, cats, love). Beginning with one participant move around the circle having the participants make up a limerick using that topic. Participant 1 provides Line 1, the next participant provides Line 2, the next participant provides Lines 3&4, and the next participant provides the final Line 5.
Example:
Part. #1 – A gentleman bought a new Ford (A)
Part. #2 – Which made his wife thoroughly bored (A)
Part. #3 – She said with a sneer (B)
        As she drank down a beer (B)
Part. #4 – Is this all that you could afford? (A)

Get new topics and start new limericks as needed.

VARIATIONS:
- Do the same game, but make the participants turn around so they face outward in the circle.
- Make it an "elimination" game where if a participant does not rhyme or ruins the rhythm they have to step out of the circle.
- Make participants sing the limericks or do them with Irish accents.

GOAL & KEYS TO SUCCESS:
Working together.
Concentration.

Limericks are often a bit naughty or silly in nature, emphasize that the logic is not as important as coming up with rhymes that work.

Remind the participant that starts the limerick that two other participants have to rhyme with the word they chose to end their line with, so it's best not to use really big words or words like "orange."

CATEGORY ELIMINATION

CATEGORY ELIMINATION (6-25 participants) is a word game designed to challenge the thinking skills of the group.

HOW TO PLAY:
Group stands in a circle facing in. The leader names a category for the group and then establishes a slow steady rhythm. Starting with any participant move around the circle clockwise, each person naming another thing in that category in rhythm, without repeating. If a participant repeats, says nothing, or breaks the rhythm, they get a strike and hold up their right hand. After each strike a new category is named. If a participant gets a 2nd strike on a subsequent category they hold up both hands, and on the 3rd strike they sit down. Play until one only participant remains.

CATEGORY IDEAS:
    Cars.
    Animals.
    Birds.
    Fast Food Restaurants.
    Ice Cream Flavors.
    Words that begin with the letter…

VARIATIONS:
• Slowly increase the speed as the number of participants dwindles.

GOAL & KEYS TO SUCCESS:
    Energy.
    Focus.
    Make sure participants speak clearly.
    Creativity.
    Friendly Competition.

CIRCLE THE BALL

CIRCLE THE BALL (6-25 participants) is a word game designed to challenge the thinking skills of the group.

HOW TO PLAY:
Group stands in a circle facing out. The leader hands a participant a ball and names a category. The participant passes the ball to his or her right and begins naming things in the category. He or she must continue naming things until the ball gets all the way around the circle back to where it started. If the participant repeats items or stops naming things before the ball gets around the circle, they must start with a new category all over again. If they are successful, they pass the ball to the next Participant and they get to name the next category.

CATEGORY IDEAS:
Cars.
Animals.
Birds.
Fast Food Restaurants.
Ice Cream Flavors.
Words that begin with the letter…

VARIATIONS:
• Keep count of how many things within a category each participant names, the one that names the most is the "Winner."

GOAL & KEYS TO SUCCESS:
Energy.
Focus.
Creativity.

Friendly Competition.

Make sure the participants in the circle pass the ball at a steady rate around the circle.

Encourage teamwork by telling the circle to pass the ball faster for hard categories.

Have the circle slow the ball down on categories with lots of answers to be named.

ABOUT THE AUTHOR

Bart Sumner is an actor, screenwriter, teacher and improv performer currently living in Grand Rapids, Michigan, with his wife Leslie, daughter Abby and two dogs. He is originally from New Jersey, and is a graduate of Rutgers University. He spent over 20 years chasing the Hollywood dream in California and has performed in films, television, musical theatre and some of the most prestigious comedy clubs in America. His son, David, died in 2009 from a severe brain injury suffered playing football. He enjoys pizza and making people laugh.

Made in the USA
Monee, IL
12 December 2019